JAVA PROGRAMMING FOR KIDS

AGES 12 - 18

Disclaimer:

The information and materials presented here are for educational purposes only. Every effort has been made to make this book as complete and as accurate as possible but no warranty or fitness is implied. The information provided is on an "as is" basis. The ideas and opinions expressed are of the author's own imagination and the author is not affiliated to any organization, school or educational discipline and will not be held accountable or liable for any inadvertent misrepresentation.

Contents

Chapter 1 : Introduction

Java is the most important programming language. If you have the full grasp of **Java** basics, then you can easily learn any object oriented programming language in this world.

What is Java?

Important points to note are:

- Java is an **object oriented programming (OOP) language**.

- Java is **platform independent** meaning that it can run on any machine containing **JVM**.

- In order to code and execute a Java code, **JDK** is needed.

What is object oriented programming or OOP?

- Object oriented programming or OOP is all about working with **classes**, **objects**, **methods** and **variables** (*explained in Chapter 3*).

- The most important concepts of OOP are: **Encapsulation**, **Inheritance** and **Polymorphism** (*explained in Chapter 7*).

What is JDK?

- **JDK** stands for **Java Development Kit** which is needed to code and execute **Java**.

- **JDK** includes both **JVM** and **JRE**.

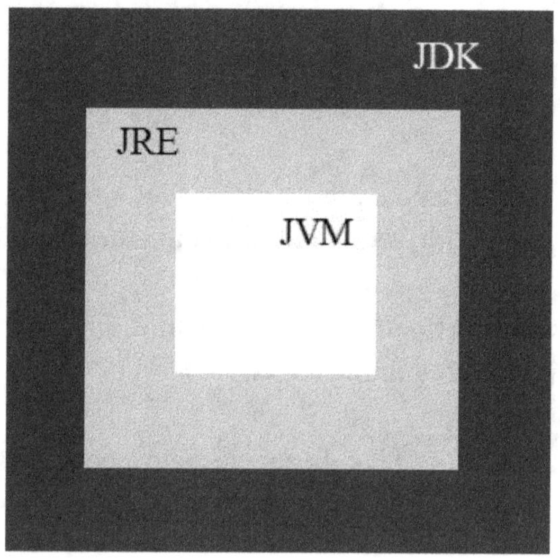

What is JRE?

- **JRE** stands for **Java Runtime Environment**.

- **JRE** contains **classes**, libraries and software that a **Java** program needs in order to run successfully.

- **JRE** also contains **JVM**.

What is JVM?

- **JVM** stands for **Java virtual machine**.

- **JVM** is responsible for converting the byte code present in .class file into machine depended code which is understood by that specific processor or operating system or machine.

JVM Architecture

Java files are saved with a **.java** extension. When we **compile** the .java file, **.class** file is generated and this **.class** file contains byte code. **JVM** handles the **.class** file and generates the desired output of the **Java** program.

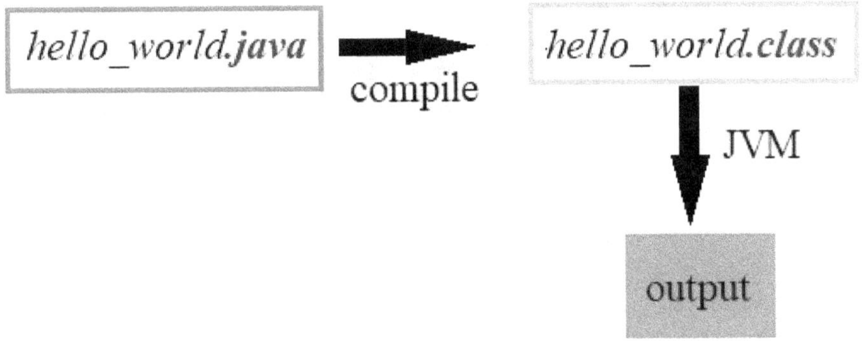

What does compilation mean in Java?

Java compilation is the process of converting a **.java** file *(which contains readable text Java code)* into a **.class** file *(which contains byte code).*

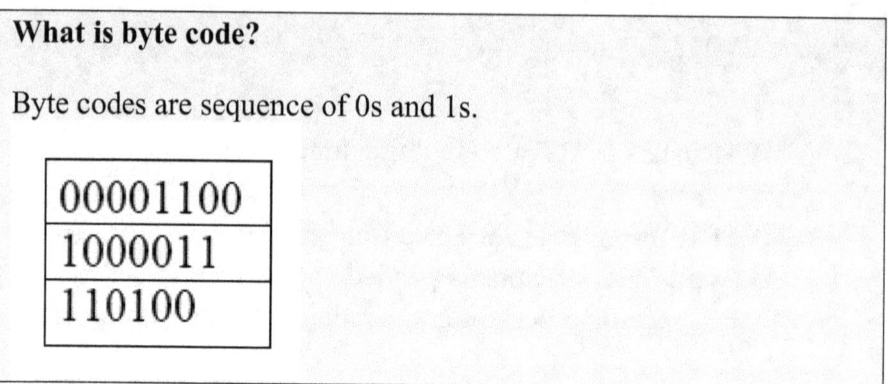

What is byte code?

Byte codes are sequence of 0s and 1s.

00001100
1000011
110100

Let's look into **JVM Architecture**.

JVM architecture is divided into three main sections:

1. Class Loader
2. JVM Memory
3. Execution Engine

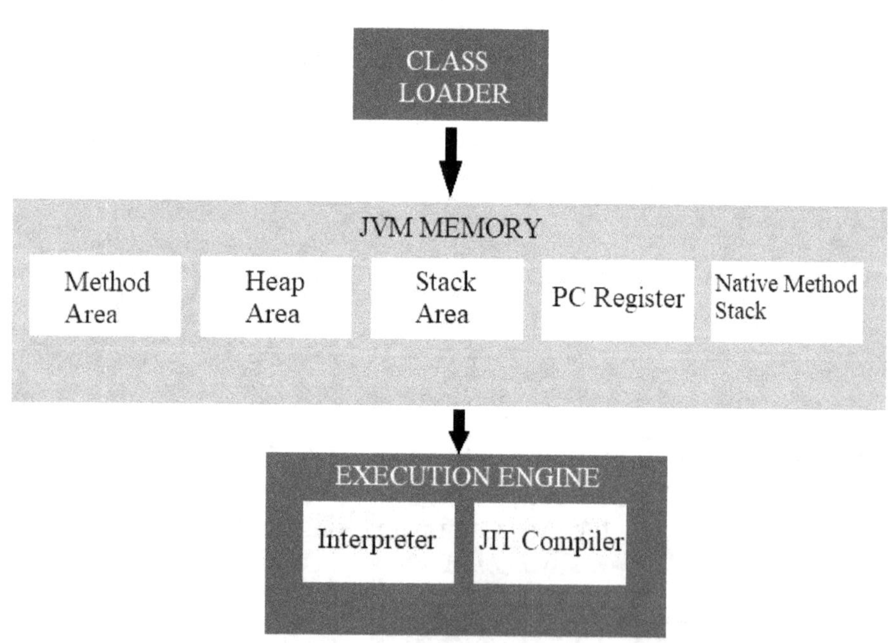

Class Loader

It is responsible for loading the **.class** file to the **JVM memory**.

JVM Memory

It is further divided into:
- **Method area** – It stores all the **method** information. (*methods explained in chapter 4*).

- **Heap area** – It stores all the **objects** and its corresponding **instance variables** (*objects and variables explained in chapter 3*).

- **Stack Area** – It stores all the **local variables** and the results of the **methods** (*local variables explained in chapter 3*).

- **PC Register** – PC register store the address of the currently executing **Java virtual machine** instruction.

- **Native Method Stacks** - Native method stacks contains native codes which are written in another language instead of **Java**.

Execution Engine

It is further divided into:
- **Interpreter** – It converts the byte code to machine dependent code which is understood by the machine and desired output is generated.

- **JIT Compiler** – JIT stands for **Just in Time** compiler and its main task is to increases the performance and efficiency of **Interpreter**.

Now let's summarize the Java program execution process

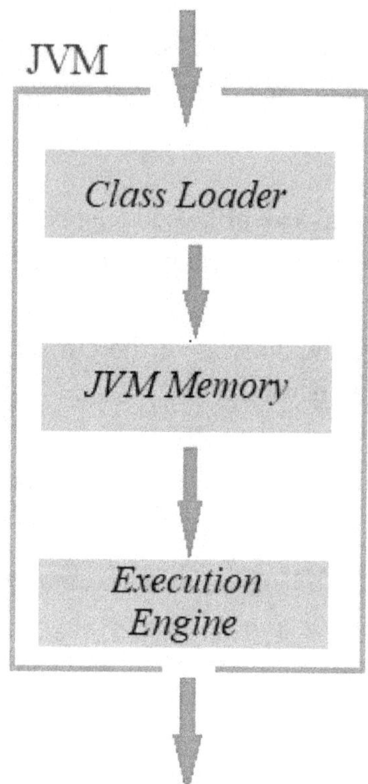

Before we start coding, we need to download and install **JDK** and an
IDE.

What is Java IDE?

IDE stands for **Integrated Development Environment**. It is a software application needed to write programs in Java.
There are multiple **IDE** present but we will be using **Eclipse IDE** to write our Java code.

Chapter 2 : Java JDK and Eclipse IDE Installation

2.1: JDK download

- Open Google chrome browser (*or any browser you like*) and search for **java jdk download** and select the **oracle website** highlighted in the screen shot below.

java jdk download

Q All   Books   Videos   News   Shopping   More

About 15,500,000 results (0.55 seconds)

www.oracle.com › java › technologies › javase-downlo…

Java SE - Downloads | Oracle Technology Network | Oracle

Oracle JDK · Oracle Customers and ISVs targeting Oracle LTS releases: Oracle JDK is supported Java SE version for customers and for developing, ...

You've visited this page 3 times. Last visit: 2/3/21

Java SE Development Kit 8
Java SE Development Kit 8 - JDK
8 - Checksum - Events - ...

Oracle JDK
Java SE Development Kit 11
Downloads · Important Oracle ...

Java SE Development Kit 15

Java SE Runtime Envir

- Download the latest **JDK** version.

Java SE 15

Java SE 15.0.2 is the latest release for the Java SE Platform

- Documentation
- Installation Instructions
- Release Notes
- Oracle License
    - Binary License
    - Documentation License
- Java SE Licensing Information User Manual
    - Includes Third Party Licenses
- Certified System Configurations

Oracle JDK

↓ JDK Download

↓ Documentation Download

- Select your operating system. (*since I am using windows, so downloading windows-x64 installer highlighted in the screen shot below*)

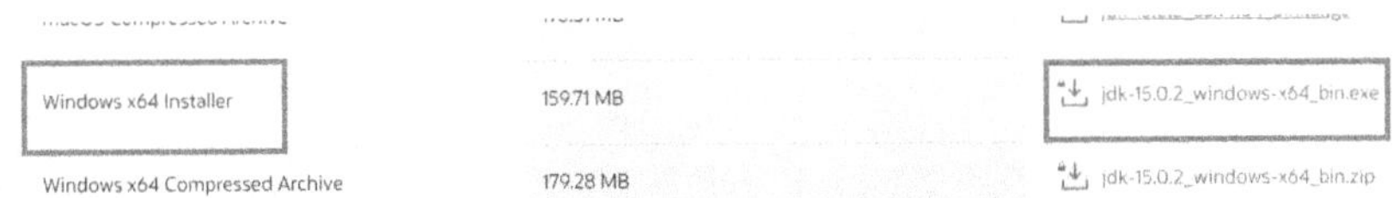

- Check on *review* box, click download and install.

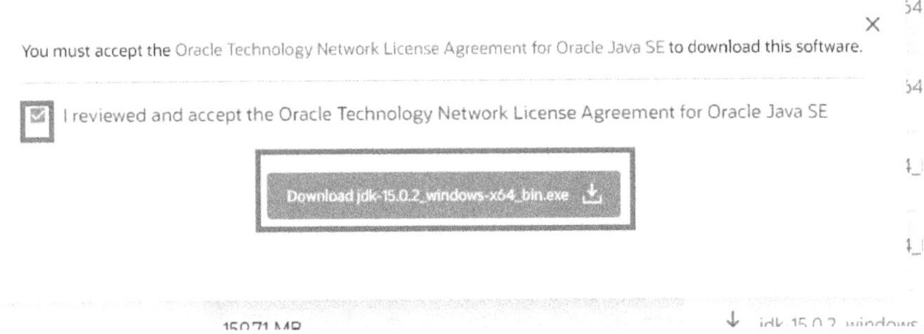

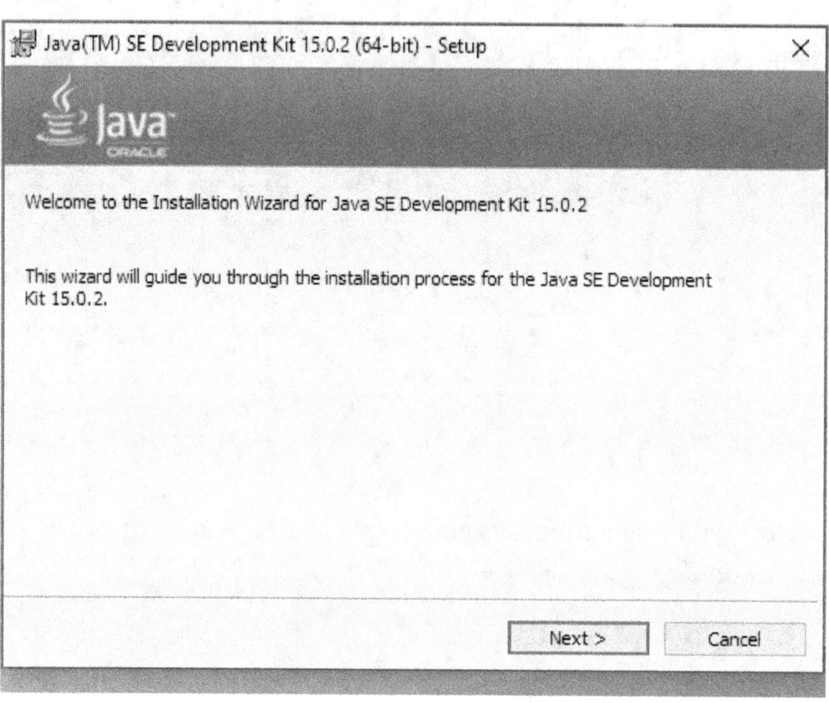

Java(TM) SE Development Kit 15.0.2 (64-bit) - Setup
Java
ORACLE
Welcome to the Installation Wizard for Java SE Development Kit 15.0.2
This wizard will guide you through the installation process for the Java SE Development Kit 15.0.2.
Next >
Cancel

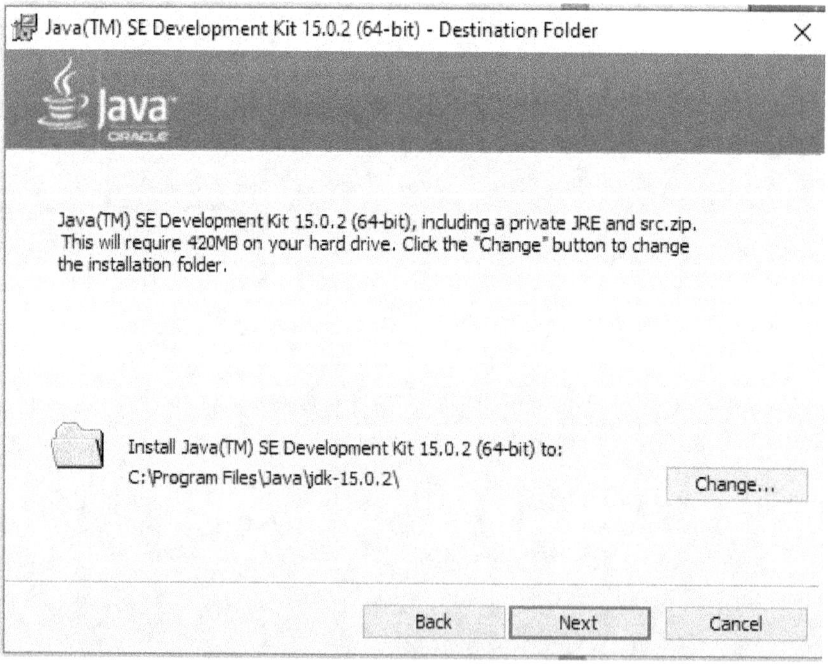

Java(TM) SE Development Kit 15.0.2 (64-bit) - Destination Folder
Java
ORACLE
Java(TM) SE Development Kit 15.0.2 (64-bit), including a private JRE and src.zip. This will require 420MB on your hard drive. Click the "Change" button to change the installation folder.
Install Java(TM) SE Development Kit 15.0.2 (64-bit) to:
C:\Program Files\Java\jdk-15.0.2\
Change...
Back
Next
Cancel

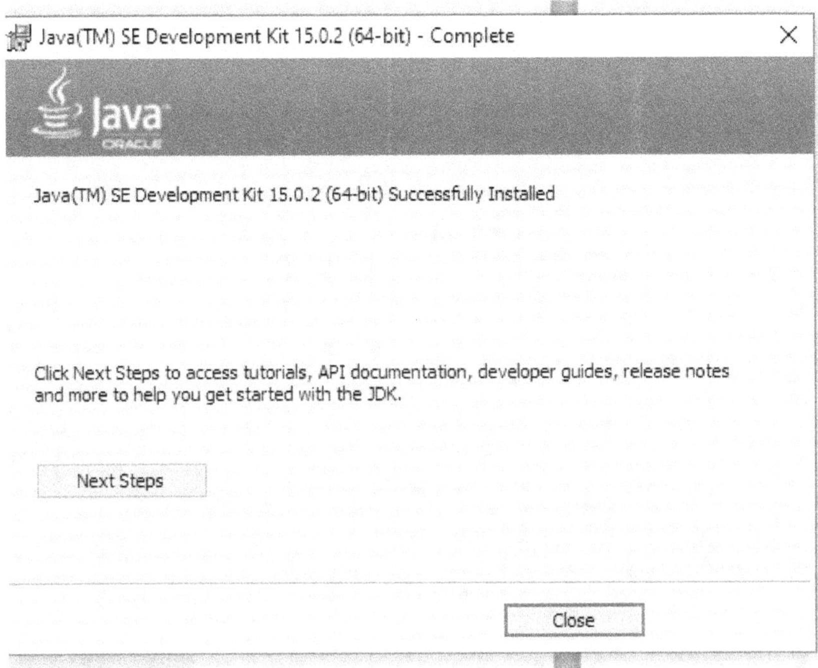

- Click close.

- Now check whether the **Java PATH** is automatically added to your **Environment Variables** or not.

What is Java PATH?

Java PATH is an environment variable which helps us to locate the **JDK bin** directory or folder which contains all the important files needed to execute a Java program.

Let's access the **Environment Variables.**

➢ Open **control panel** -> click on **System and Security**.

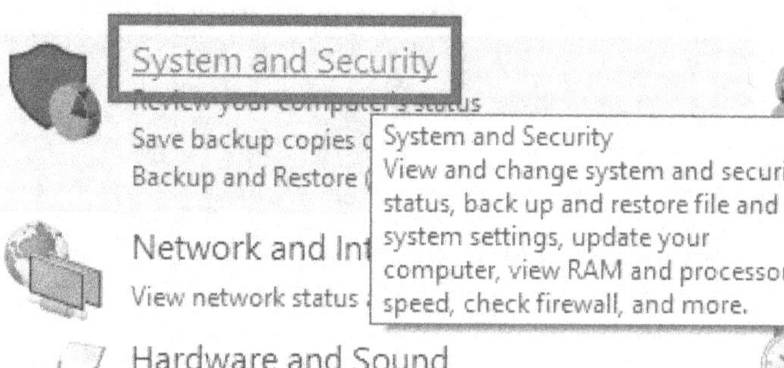

> ➢ Click on **System**

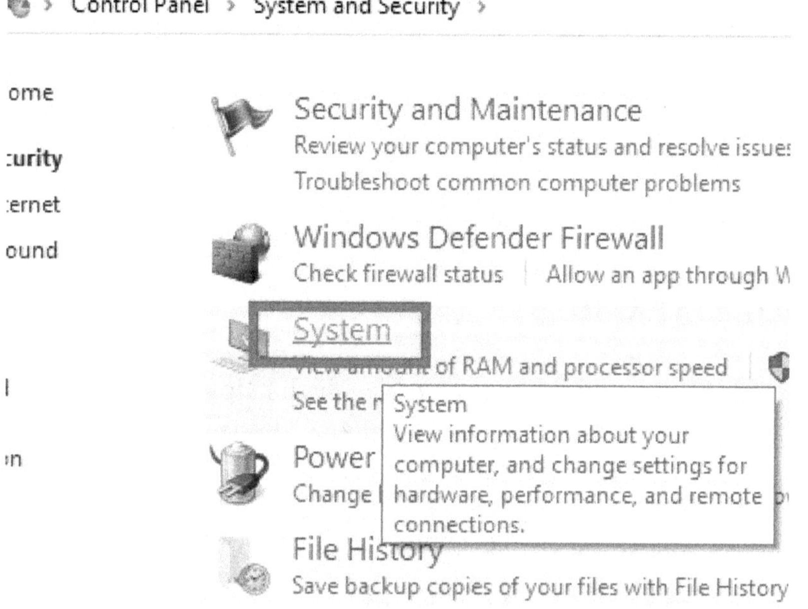

> ➢ Click on **Advanced system settings.**

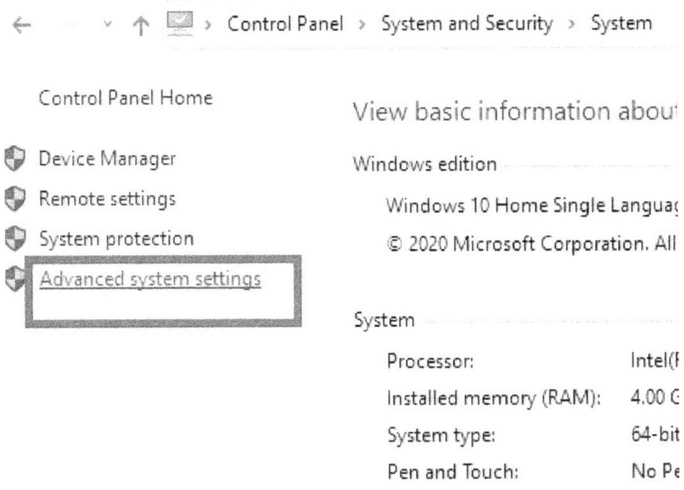

> ➤ Click on **Environment Variables.**

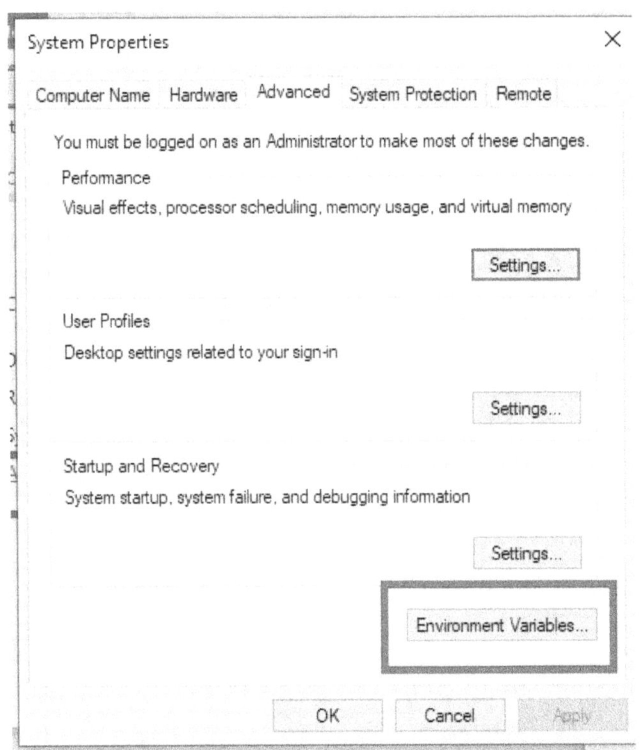

➢ Under **System variables**, select **Path** -> click **Edit**

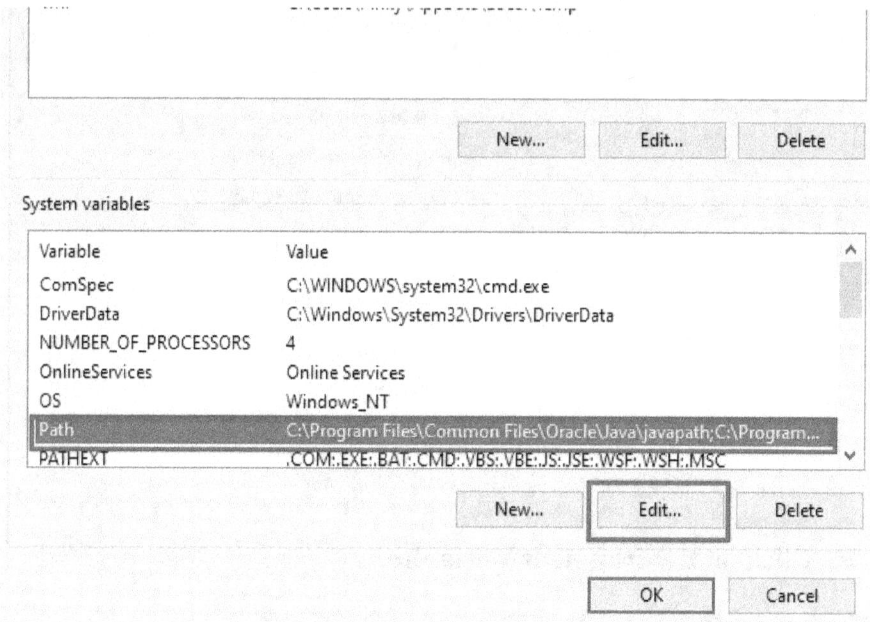

➢ **Javapath** shows highlighted in the screen shot below.

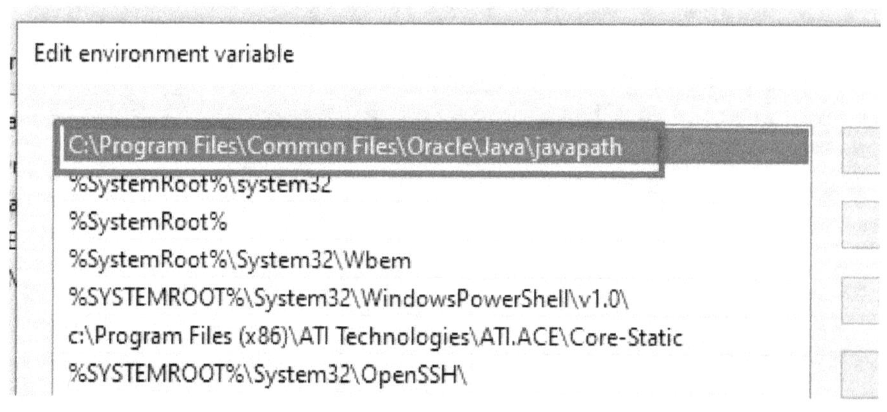

➢ Click ok and exit.

We have successfully installed **JDK** in our machine. Now let's download and install **Eclipse IDE.**

2.2: Download and install Eclipse IDE

- Go to website https://www.eclipse.org/downloads/packages/ and download the latest version of **Eclipse IDE**.
  (*since I am using windows operating system, so downloaded Eclipse IDE for Windows*)

Eclipse IDE 2020-12 R Packages

Eclipse IDE for Java Developers

921 MB   776.300 DOWNLOADS

The essential tools for any Java developer, including a Java IDE, a Git client, XML Editor, Maven and Gradle integration

Windows x86_64
macOS x86_64
Linux x86_64 | AArch64

Eclipse IDE for Enterprise Java Developers

/ Downloads / Eclipse downloads - Select a mirror

downloads are provided under the terms and conditions of the Eclipse Foundation Software User Agreement unless otl ecified.

⬇ Download

Download from: Canada - Rafal Rzeczkowski (https)

File: eclipse-java-2020-12-R-win32-x86_64.zip SHA-512

>> Select Another Mirror

- After finish downloading, open the download folder in your machine.

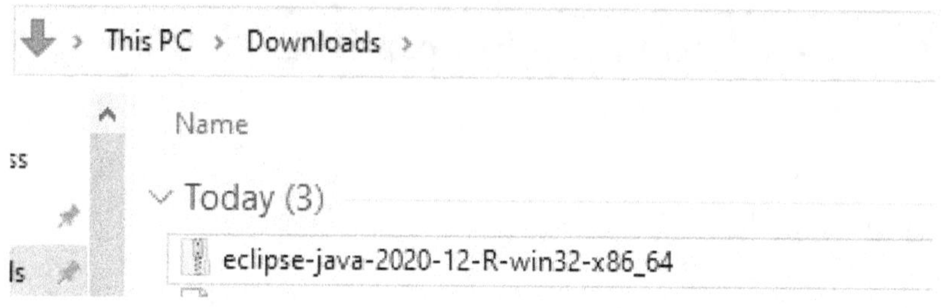

The downloaded folder is a ZIP folder and we need to extract it in order to access **Eclipse** application.
So right click on ZIP folder and click **extract all.**

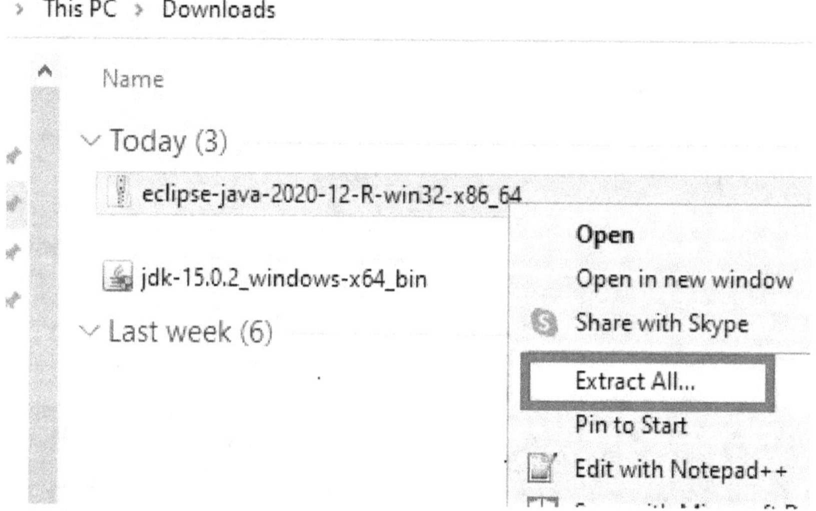

Browse for your extract location and click on **Extract**.

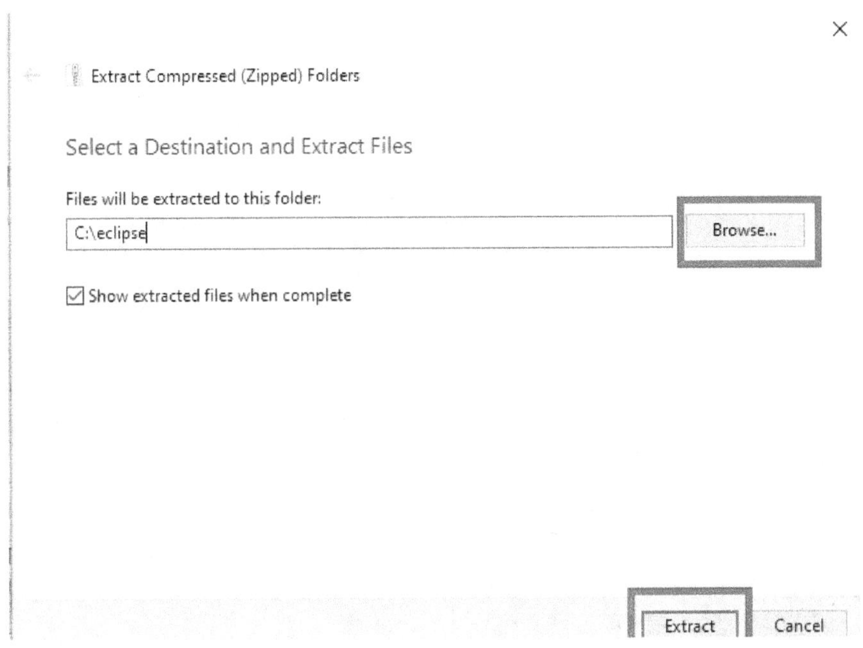

Now open the **eclipse** folder and look for the **eclipse application** highlighted in the screen shot below.

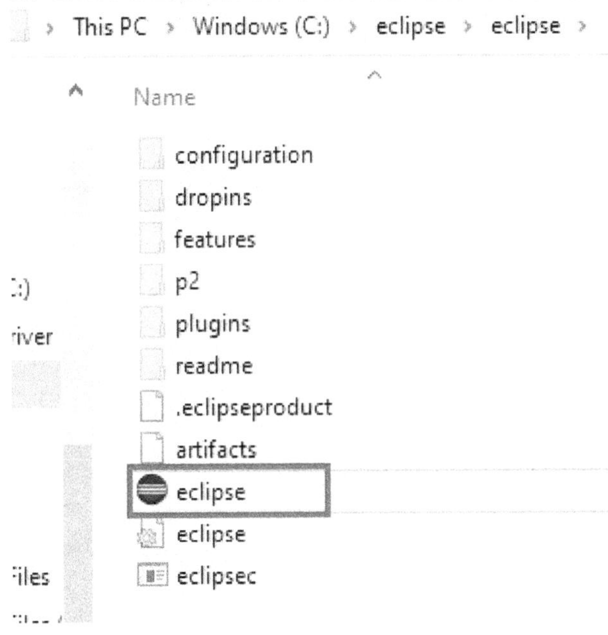

Click and open the **eclipse** application.

Select a **workspace** and click on **launch**

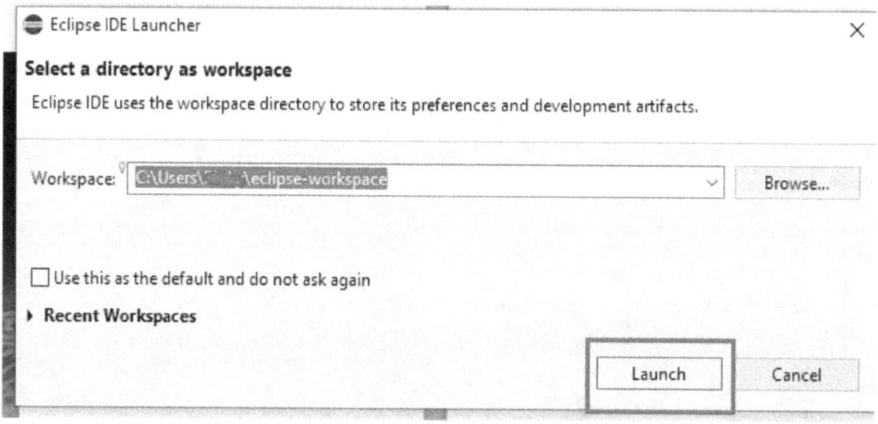

We have now successfully installed **Eclipse IDE**.

Let's begin coding..

Chapter 3 : Class, Object, Variables and Data types

3.1: What is a Java Class & Object?

Class

Important points to note are:

- **Java class** is a blueprint for creating an **object**.

- **Java class** contains **methods** and **variables**.

- The syntax for creating a **Java class** is:

```
access_modifier class class_name {
.........
}
```

Object

- An **object** instance of a **class**.

- An **object** contains the copy of **methods** and **variables** present inside its **class**.

- The syntax for creating a **Java object** is:

```
type object_name = new class_name ( )
```
The **type** denotes the type of **object** declared.

The **new** keyword is used to create an **object**.

The **new** keyword is followed by call to a **constructor** *(constructor explained in chapter 4).*

For example: *Animal a = new Animal( ),* here *a* is an **object** of type *Animal* **(Class name)** and the **new** keyword is followed by call to *Animal* **default constructor**.

I know it all sounds extremely complicated, let's try to simplify a little bit below.

Let us consider a class room containing three students, *John, Ram* and *Katy*. These three students have few things in common and they are as follows:

1. All three are students of a class room.
2. They each have a name.
3. They each have a student_ID.
4. They each have an age.
5. They each have a gender.
6. They each have their home address.

These six things listed above are called **attributes** of a student. In **Java** world, we can depict these **attributes** in the form of a **variable**.

A student performs multiple functions like studying, eating, playing etc. In **Java** world, these **functions** can be depicted by **methods.**

We have successfully stated the **attributes** and **functions** of a Student. Now the big question is where we can store these information?. Well we can store this information in a **class.**

The students *John, Ram* and *Katy* have their own individual characteristics and they all fall under the student category. In **Java** world, these three students are referred as **objects** of **class** *student* and the **objects** will contain a copy of all **variables** and **methods** declared within its **class.**

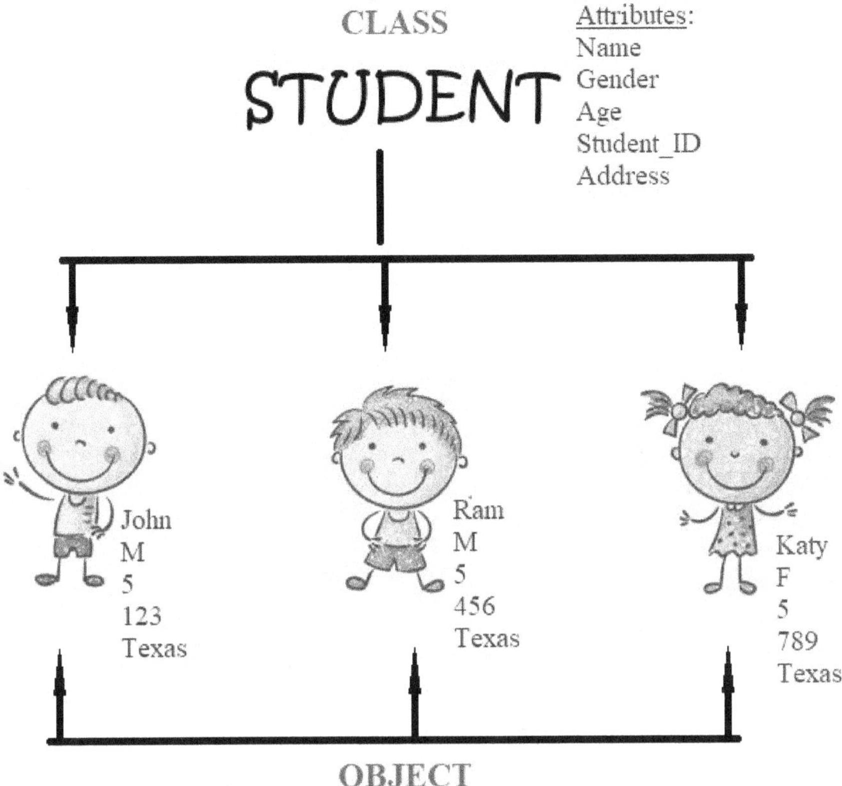

Let's summarize the concept:

- **Student** is a **class.**
- *John*, *Ram* and *Katy* are **objects** which belong to **class Student**.
- Name, Gender, Age, Student_ID, Address are **variables** of **class Student**.

We will look into another example of **Java class** and **object.**

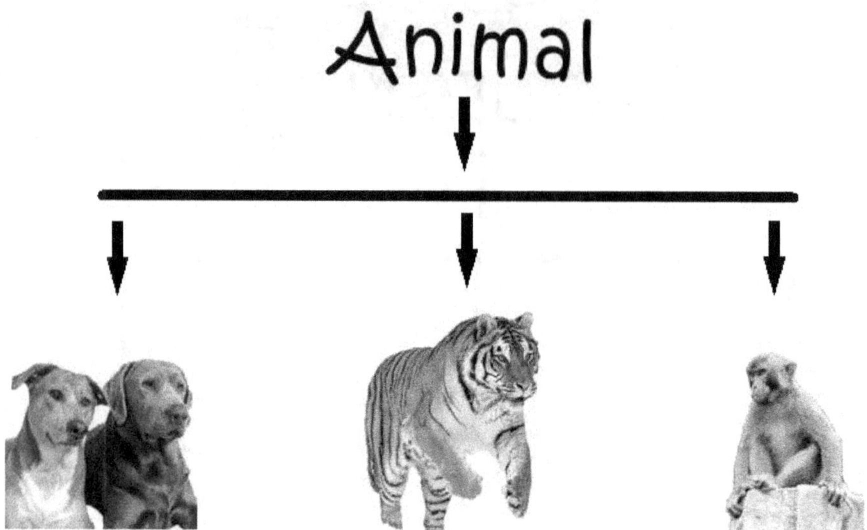

There are multiple animals which belong to the animal kingdom. There are *dogs, tigers, monkeys, lion* etc. All animals have few things in common like they all fall under the animal category, they all have a name, weight, age and they also perform some common functions like eating, playing and many more.

In **Java** world, we can write all the above information in a **class** *Animal* and the **objects** of **class** *Animal* will be *dog, tiger , monkey*.

In other words we can say an **object** is a small miniscule entity of the vast **class** which has its own properties and characteristic.

3.2: What is Java Variable?

Important points to note are:
- **Java variables** act as a container to hold data.

- The **variables** are declared with a **Data type**.

Example: **int** *age*

Here *age* is a **variable** name whose **data type** is int or integer meaning that the **variable** *age* can hold only numeric whole numbers.

Java variables are of three types:

1. **Local variable** – These **variables** are declared within **methods** *(methods discussed in chapter 4)* and the **variables** get destroyed soon after exiting the **method**.

2. **Instance variable** – These **variables** are declared within the **class**.

3. **Static variables** – The values of these **variables** remains **constant** or **static** and it also does not require any **object** to access it.

3.3: Java Data Types

Java data types are divided into two categories:

1. **Primitive Data Type** – It contains boolean, char, int, short, byte, long, float, and double.

2. **Non-Primitive Data Type**: It contains String, Array, etc.

Data type	Description
int	This data type stores integer values like 1,2,3,4 ….50..80

float	This data type stores fractional numbers like 123.50
char	This data type stores a single character value like '*A*' or '*B*' or '*C*'
boolean	This data type returns TRUE or FALSE of any given expression or condition.
String	String is a Java **class** which is used to stores group of characters. Example: "*John*" or "*Hello students*" etc

In the above ***Student* class** example of section 3.1:

- **Variable *Name*** will be of data types **String.**

- **Variable *Gender*** is usually denoted by a single character M *(for male)* or F *(for female)* so its data types will be **char.**

- **Variable *Age*** will be of data type **int.**

- **Variable *Student_ID*** may contain numbers and character values together, so let's assign a data type of **String** to it.

- **Variable *Address*** will be of data types **String.**

3.4: What are access modifiers?

Access modifiers denote the accessibility of a **class** or a **method**. It is broadly divided into 4 types:

1: **Public access modifiers** – This means that the **class** or **method** is accessible from everywhere.

2: **Private access modifiers** – This means that the **class** or **method** is accessible only from within.

3: **Default access modifiers** – This means that the **class** or **method** is accessible only from within its **package**.

4: **Protected access modifiers** – This means that the **class** or **method** is accessible from within its **package** or any **package** other than its own **package** through **inheritance** only *(inheritance discussed in chapter 7)*.

3.5: What is Java package?

- A **Java package** contain group of **Java classes**.

- **Java packages** are mainly done to avoid name conflicts.
  If a **package** contains two **Java class** files of the same name, it will lead to name conflict and error in the **Java** project may occur in future. In order to prevent that from happening, separate **packages** should be created for storing the **class** file which has the same name.

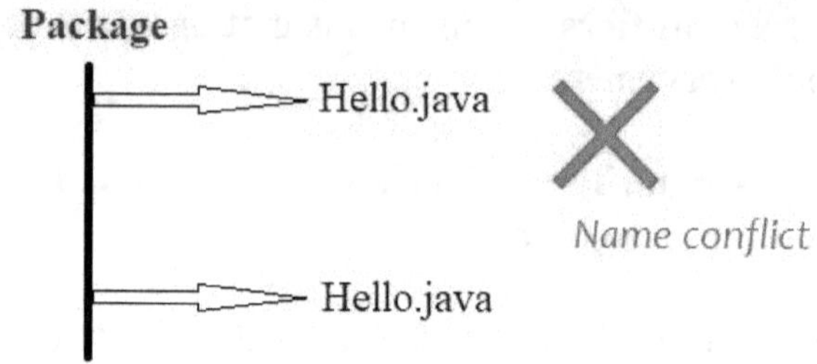

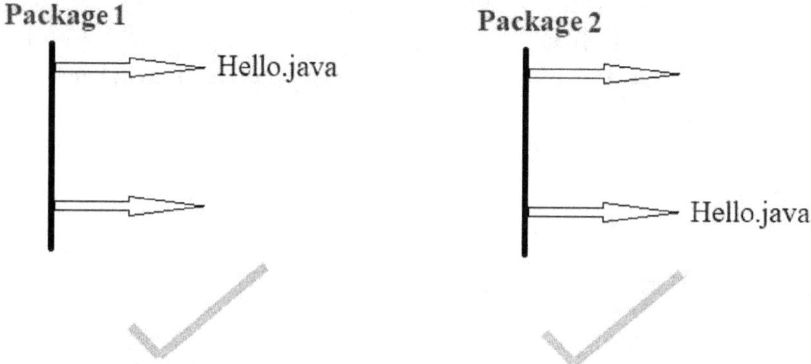

Now let's code..

3.6: Examples

<u>Example 1</u>

Launch **Eclipse IDE** and create a new **Java project**.

- Click on **File -> New -> Java Project**.

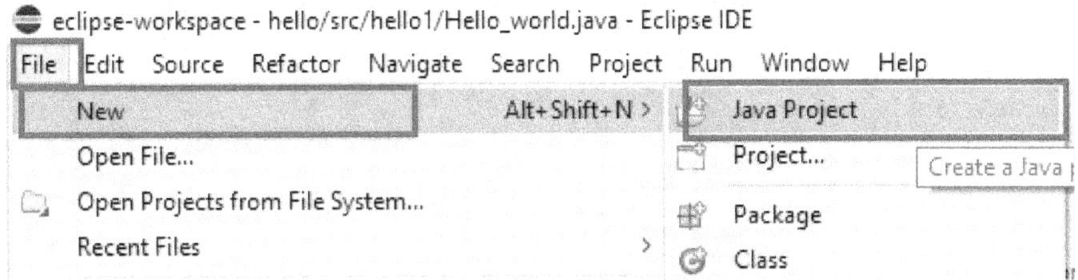

- Give the **Project name** (*I named **hello_world***) and click on **Finish**.

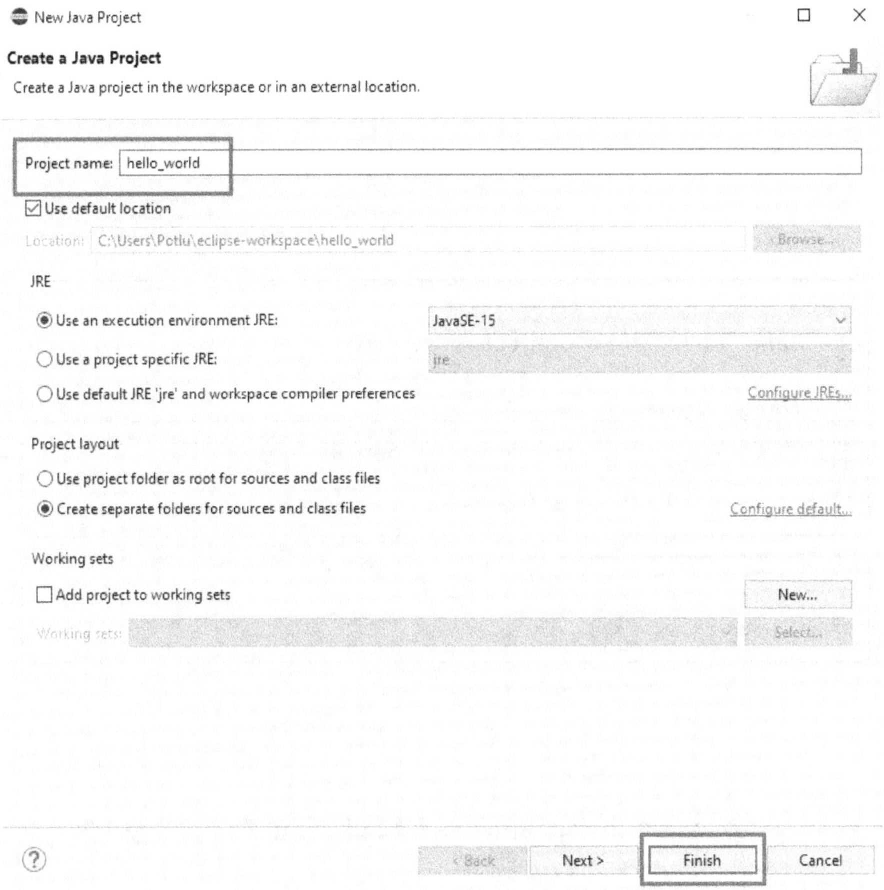

- On **Create module-info.java** window, for now I will be clicking on *Don't Create*.

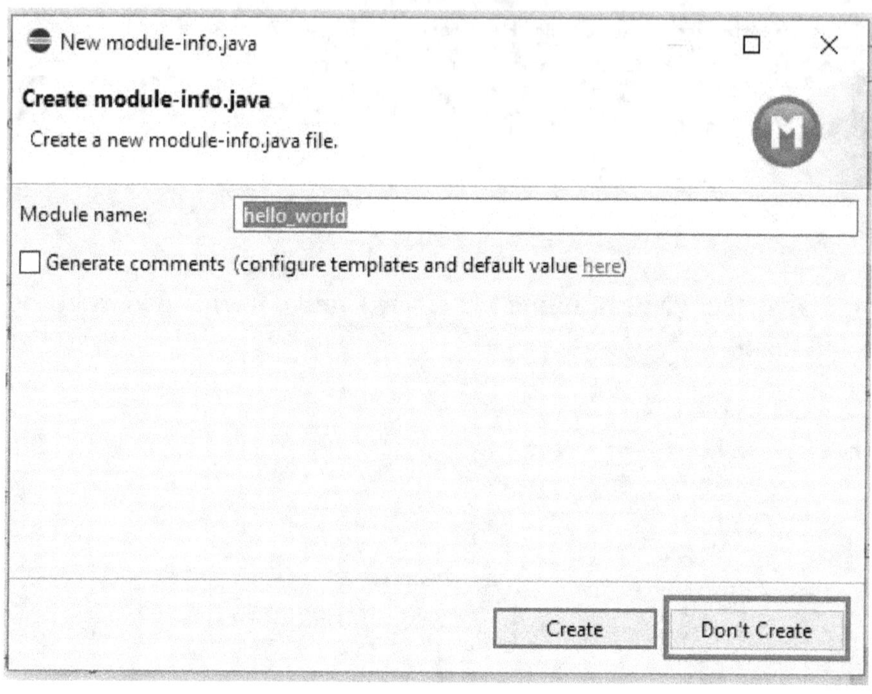

Our *hello_world* **Java project** is created.

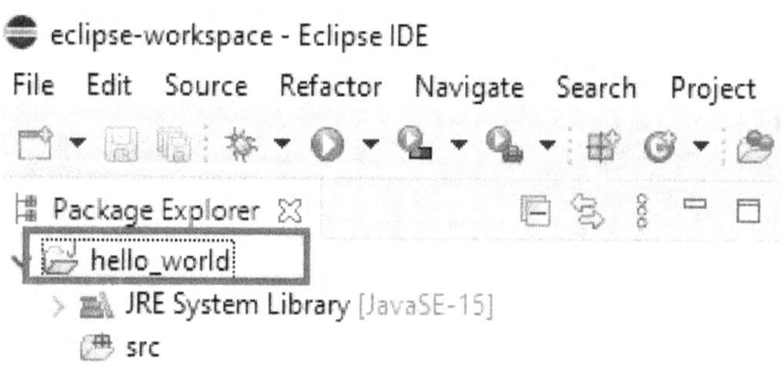

- Right click on the **src** folder -> Click **New** -> **Package** *(we are creating a new package)*.

What is the default src folder of Eclipse IDE?

Default src folder is the source folder which contains the source code or the main code of our project.

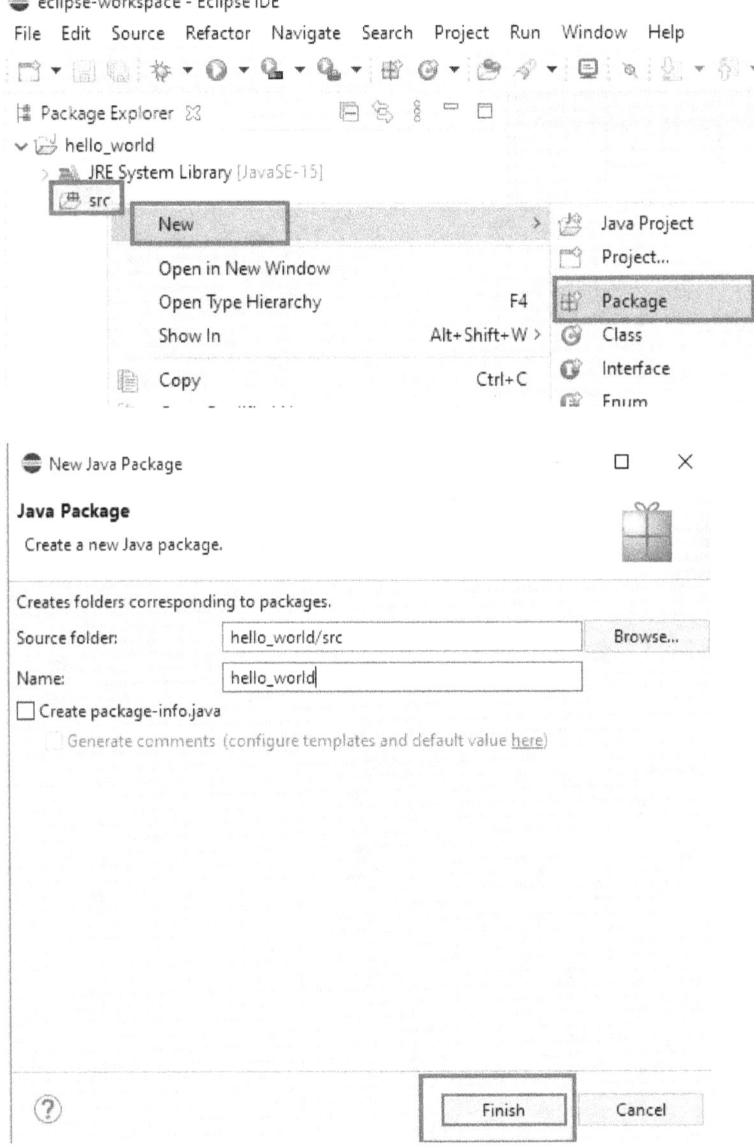

Click Finish

- Right click on the ***hello_world*** **package** -> click **New** -> Click **Class** (*we are creating a new Java **class***)

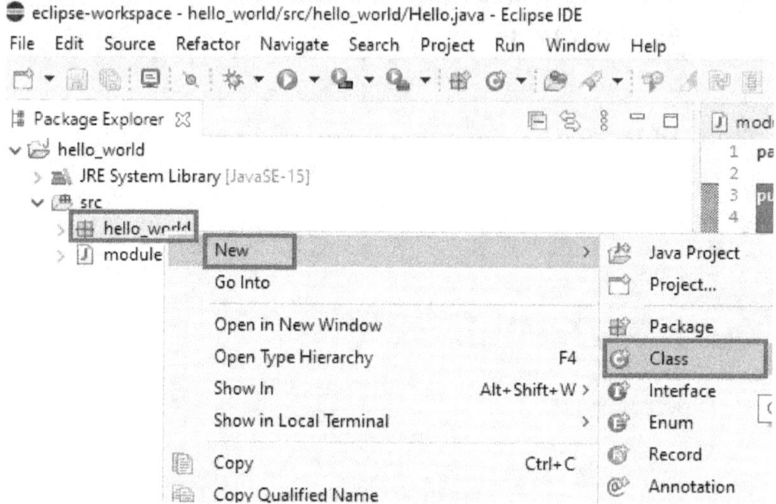

Give the **Class** name (*I gave **Hello***) starting with a capital letter -> check on **public static void main(String[] args)** box -> click **Finish**.

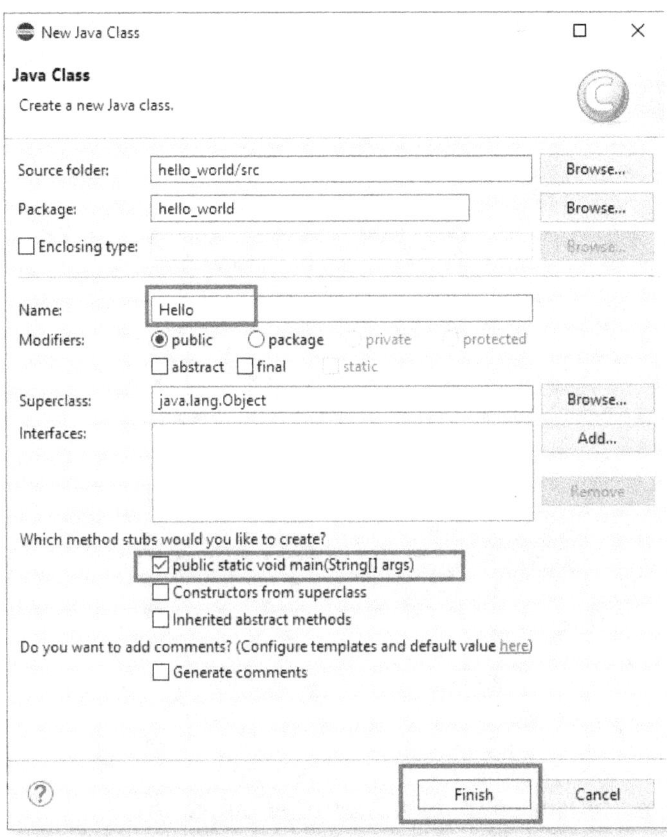

- In *Hello.java*, write one line of code highlighted in the screen shot below and execute the program by clicking on the **run** button.

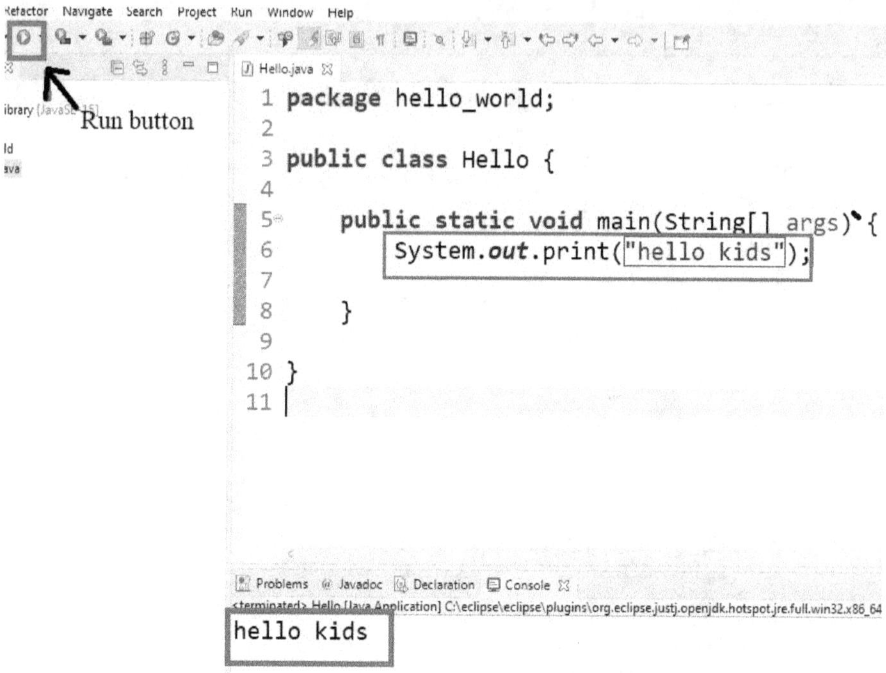

Code explanation:

- **System.out.print** is used to display or print output. **System.put.println** is same as **System.out.print** but the **println** displays output in separate lines.

- At line 5, you will notice a very important line of code that is **public static void main(String[] args)**. It is the **Java main method** and it acts as an entry point to our **Java** Program. Any Java program will only start execution process after it encounters this very important line of code. *(We will discuss more about this line of code in Chapter 4).*

Example 2

Let's create another **Java class**.

- Right click on *hello_world* **package** -> **New** -> **Class** *(I named my class file **students**)*

- In ***students.java***, write the following lines of code.

```java
1 package hello_world;
2
3 public class Students {
4
5     String name;
6
7
8     public static void main(String[] args) {
9         Students student1 = new Students();
10        Students student2 = new Students();
11        Students student3 = new Students();
12
13        student1.name = "John";
14        student2.name = "Ram";
15        student3.name = "Katy";
16
17        System.out.println(student1.name);
18        System.out.println(student2.name);
19        System.out.println(student3.name);
20    }
21 }
```

Code explanation:

- At line 5, we declared an instance variable *(explained in section 3.2)* **name** whose data type *(explained in section 3.3)* is String.

- At line 8, the very important line of code **public static void main(String[] args)** is written.

> **Please Note:** Always remember **Java objects** must be declared only after typing this very important line of code.

- At line 9, 10, 11 different **objects** of **class *Students*** are created.

- With the help of **dot (.) operator**, we access the **variable *name*** from **class *Students.***

- At line 13, 14, 15, we pass values or data into the ***name* variable** of each **object**.

- At line 17, 18, 19, we print out the values.

Now let's run the above piece of code

Problems @ Javadoc Declaration Console
<terminated> Students [Java Application] C:\eclipse\eclipse\plug

```
John
Ram
Katy
```

Chapter 4: Constructors & Methods

In previous chapter we learnt about the basic idea of a **method**. In this chapter we will create a **Java** program containing **constructors** and **methods**.

4.1: Constructor

We learnt about **Java object** syntax in chapter 3, section 3.1 and we learnt that the **new** keyword is followed by call to a **constructor** so **what is Java constructor?**.

- **Java constructor** is a special **Java method** that is used to initialize **Java objects**.

- **Java constructor's** name must match with the **Java class** name.

- **Java constructor** does not have a **return type** *(return type discussed in section 4.2)*.

- **Java constructor** is always called during **object** creation. If a **class** does not contain any **constructor**, then **Java compiler** automatically created a **default constructor** and executes the program.

Java constructor is of two types:

1. Default constructor

2. Parameterized constructor

Default constructor

Default constructor does not contain any **parameter**.

Parameterized constructor

Parameterized constructor contains **parameters**.

What is parameter?

Parameter is a **variable** which is passed to a **method** or **constructor**. A **method** or **constructor** can have one **parameter** or multiple **parameters**.

Example

➢ Launch **Eclipse IDE** -> create a new **class** (*I named my class Multiply)*

```java
1  package hello_world;
2
3  public class Multiply {
4      int value1, value2;
5
6      Multiply() {
7          // default constructor
8      }
9
10     Multiply(int x, int y) {
11         // parameterized constructor
12         value1 = x;
13         value2 = y;
14     }
15
16     public int multiply() {
17         int z = value1 * value2;
18         return z;
19     }
20
21     public static void main(String[] args) {
22         Multiply m = new Multiply(10, 10);
23         System.out.println(m.multiply());
24
25     }
26
27 }
```

Code explanation:

- At line 4, **instance variable** (*instance variable discussed in chapter 3, section 3.2*) ***value1*** and ***value 2*** are declared.

- At line 6, we created our **default constructor**.

- At line 10, we created our **parameterized constructor** and it takes two **parameters** *x* and *y*.

- At line 12, we passed *x* to ***value1*** meaning that when we will assign a value to **variable *x*,** that value will in turn get assigned to **variable *value1*.**

- At line 13, we passed *y* to ***value2*** meaning that when we will assign a value to **variable *y*,** that value will in turn get assigned to **variable *value2*.**

- At line 16, **method *multiply*** is declared and this **method** will return the multiplication result.

- At line 21, Java **main method** is declared *(we have discussed about this very important line of code in chapter 3 and we will discuss more about this method as we proceed further).*

- At line 22, **object *m*** is created and values are passed to ***Multiply*** constructor *(parameterized constructor created in line 10. Value 10 is assigned to **instance variable value1** and other value 10 is assigned to **value2)***

- At line 23, **method *multiply*** is called.

Now let's run the above piece of code

```
Problems  @ Javadoc  Declaration  Console
<terminated> Multiply [Java Application] C:\eclipse\eclipse\pluc
100
```

4.2: Method

- A **Java method** is a block of code performing some task.

  For example: Let us consider a **Math class**, **Math** contains numbers and with those numbers we can perform multiple **functions** like addition, subtraction, multiplication, division etc. In **Java**, we can write these **functions** in a **method**.

- The **signature** of a **Java method** is:

  access_modifier return_type *method_name* {

  ....

  }

(**access_modifier** *discussed in section 3.4 of chapter 3*)

What is return type in Java?

Return type is the **data type** of the value returned by the **method**. Example: Let us consider the **method signature** written below:

public int *addition* ( ) {
}
In the above **method signature**, the **method**'s name is *addition* and its return type is **int**. This means that the *addition* **method** will return a value of data type **int**.
In order to return the value of a **method return keyword** is used.

Let us consider another **method signature** written below:

public void *show*( ) {
}
In the above **method signature**, the **method**'s name is *show* and its return type is **void**. This means that the *show* **method** will return no value.

<u>**Example**</u>

- Launch **Eclipse IDE** -> create a new **Class** within the *hello_world* **package** (*created in chapter 3*)
  (I named my **Class** *Math)*

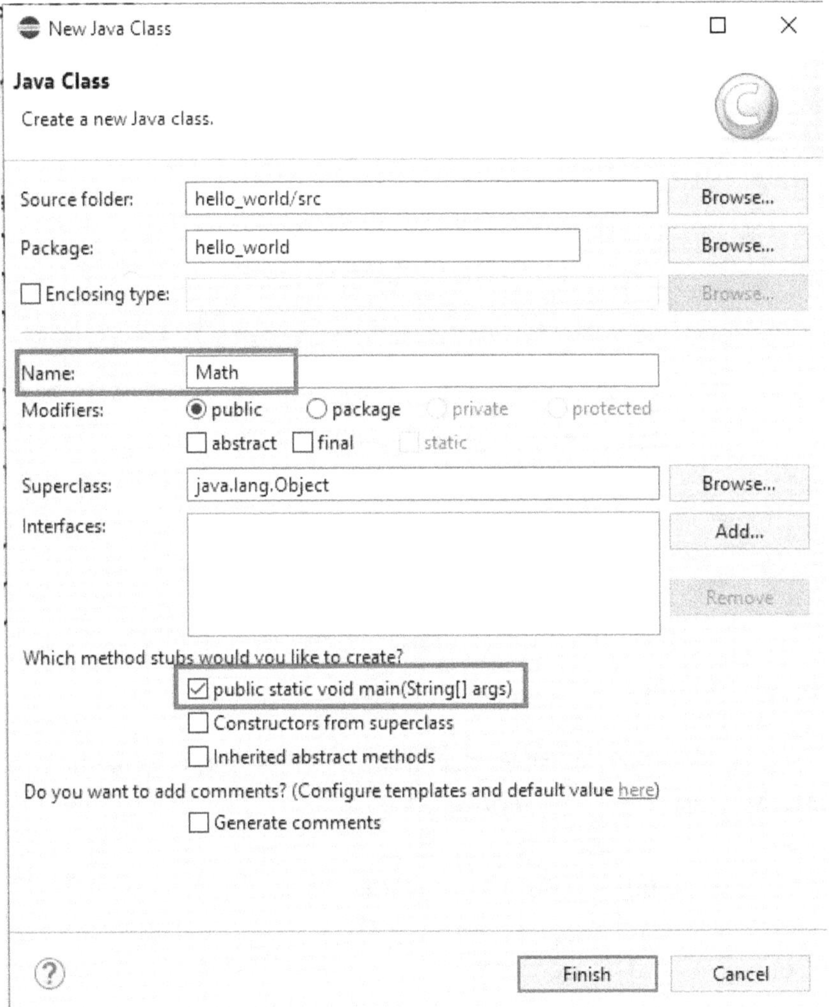

- In ***Math.java*** write the following lines of code.

```java
1 package hello_world;
2
3 public class Math {
4
5      public int addition(int x, int y) {
6          int z;
7          z = x + y;
8          return z;
9      }
10
11     public int subtraction(int x, int y) {
12          int z;
13          z = x - y;
14          return z;
15      }
16
17     public static void main(String[] args) {
18
19          Math m = new Math();
20          System.out.println(m.addition(10, 10));
21          System.out.println(m.subtraction(10, 5));
22
23      }
24
25 }
```

Code explanation:

- At Line 3, *Math* **class** is declared and this **class** contains two **methods** *addition* and *subtraction*.

- At line 5, *addition* **method** is declared.

  Let's look into its signature.

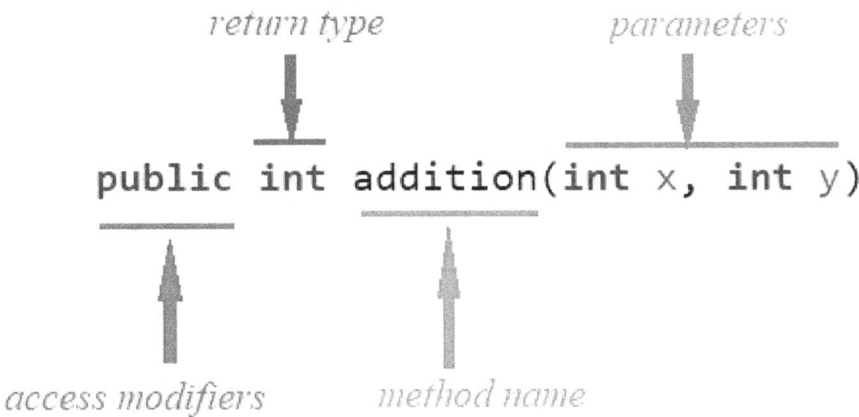

- o At line 6, we declared a **local variable** *z* *(local variable discussed in chapter 3, section 3.2).*

- o At line 7, we perform the arithmetic operation.

- o At line 8, we return the value of *z* with the help of **return keyword**.

- Line 11 – 14, contains **method *subtraction*** and it follows the same process of **method *addition*.**

- Line 17 contains the main line of code which will start the execution process and will act as an entry point to ***Math.java***.

- At line 19, **object *m*** of **class *Math*** is created. This **object** will contain a copy of all **methods** and **variables** of **class *Math*.** In order to access those information **dot (.) operator** is used.

- At line 20 and 21, the **methods** of **class *Math*** are accessed and **arguments** are passed into those **methods** *(In **addition method**, value 10 is assigned to **variable x** and other value 10 is assigned* *to **variable y**. In **subtraction method,** the value 10 is assigned to **variable x** and other value 5 is assigned to **variable y)**.* Then the results of those **methods** are printed by **System.out.println**.

What is Argument?

Arguments are data values which are passed to the **method parameters**.

Now let's run the above piece of code

```
Problems  @ Javadoc  Declaration  Console

<terminated> Math [Java Application] C:\eclipse\eclipse\plugins\
20
5
```

4.3: What is public static void main (String[ ] args)?

We have learnt in chapter 3 as well as in this chapter that **public static void main (String[ ] args)** is the most important line of code in any **Java** program. This line of code acts as an entry point or starting point of any **Java** program.

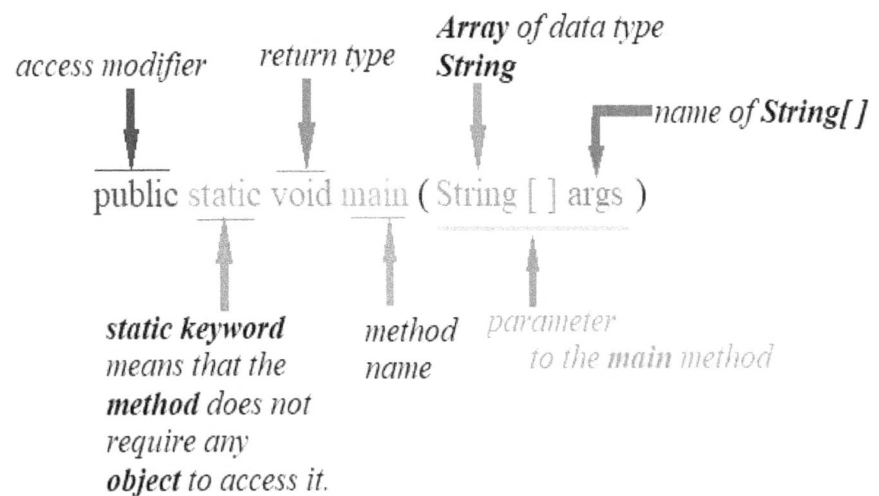

Please Note: JVM accesses the **Java main method**. *(JVM discussed in chapter 1)*

4.4: Mathematical Operators in Java

Arithmetic Operator	Description
+	Addition
-	Subtraction
*	Multiplication
/	Division

%	Returns the Division remainder
++	Increments a **variable** by 1. Example $x = x + 1$. If value of x is 5, then the new value of x will be $5 + 1 = 6$.
--	Decrements a **variable** by 1. Example $x = x - 1$. If value of x is 4, then the new value of x will be $4 - 1 = 3$.

Chapter 5: Conditional Statements & Loops

5.1: Conditional Statements

- **Java** contains multiple conditional statements and they are:

  1. **if**
  2. **else**
  3. **else if**

- The syntax of **if** and **else** is:

  ```
  if ( condition ) {
  ...............code.........
  }
  else {
  ............... code ...................
  }
  ```

- The syntax of **if**, **else if** and **else** is:

  ```
  if ( condition ) {
  ........code....................
  }
  else if ( condition ) {
  ...........code...................
  }
  ```

```
else {
.....................code...............
}
```

These conditional statements check where a certain condition returns Boolean value **TRUE** or **FALSE**. If the condition returns **TRUE**, a block of code executes, else another block of code executes.

<u>Execution flow of if and else</u>

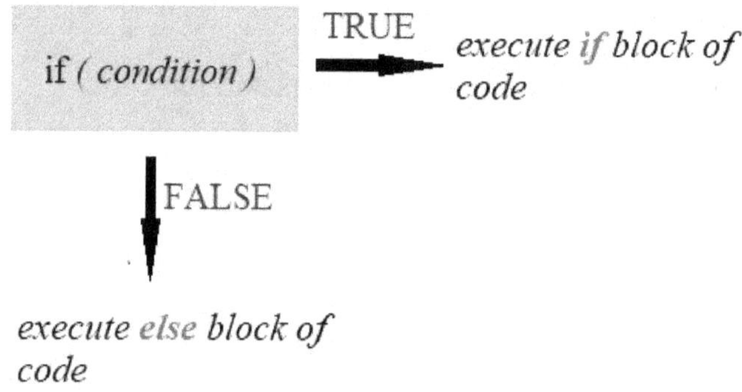

<u>Execution flow of if, else if and else</u>

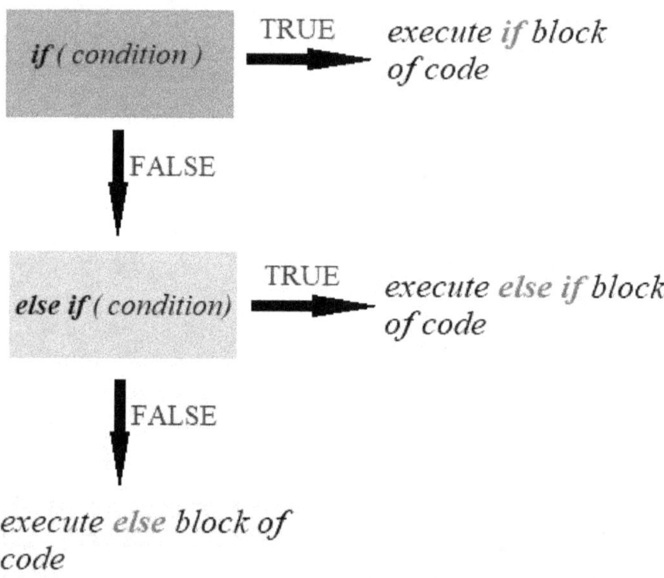

<u>**Logical operations available in Java**</u>

Operator	Description
x > y	Checks whether the value of x is greater than the value of y
x < y	Checks whether the value of x is less than the value of y
x == y	Checks whether value of x is equal to the value of y
x != y	Checks whether the value of x is NOT equal to the value of y
x >= y	Checks whether the value of x is greater than and equal to the value of y
x <= y	Checks whether the value of x is less than and equal to the value of y

Let's code..

<u>**Example**</u>

- Launch **Eclipse IDE** and create a new **Java Class** *(I named my class **ConditionalStatements**)* and write the following lines of code shown in the screen shot below.

```java
1 package hello_world;
2
3 public class ConditionalStatements {
4
5     public static void main(String[] args) {
6
7             int x = 5;
8             int y = 10;
9
10            if (x > y) {
11                System.out.println("x is greater");
12            }
13            else if (x == y) {
14                System.out.println("x is equal to y");
15            }
16            else {
17                System.out.println("x is less than y");
18            }
19
20        }
21
22 }
```

Code explanation:

- At line 3, **Class *ConditionalStatements*** is declared.

- At line 5, **public static void main (String[ ] args)** is written (*this line of code was discussed in chapter 3 and chapter 4*).

- At lines 7 and 8, **instance variables** (*discussed in section 3.2 of chapter 3*) *x* and *y* are declared and values 5 and 10 are assigned to it.

- At line 10, **if condition** is declared. It checks whether the value of *x* is greater than the value of *y*. If the condition is satisfied or return Boolean value **TRUE**, line 11 executes.

- At line 13, **else if condition** is declared. It checks whether the value of *x* is equal to the value of *y*. If both values are equal, line 14 executes.

- At line 16, **else** condition is declared and this block of code runs if both **if** and **else if** condition is not satisfied.

*In this example, the value of x is 5 and the value of y is 10, so the value of x is not greater than the value of y and hence the condition will return **FALSE** and line 11 will not execute. The value of x is obviously not equal to the value of y, so the condition will return **FALSE** and the line 14 will not execute.*
*Value of x was not greater than y (stated in **if** condition) and value of x was not equal to the value of y (stated in **else if** condition), so this means that x is less than y and **else** block of code executes.*

Now let's run the above piece of code.

Problems   @ Javadoc   Declaration   Console
<terminated> ConditionalStatements [Java Application] C:\eclipse\eclipse\pl

```
x is less than y
```

5.2: Loops

- There are two types of loop:

    1. for loop

2. while loop

These loops are used to loop through a block of code to test whether a certain condition is satisfied or not.

- **for loop** works best with **Arrays** (*we will learn about Array basics in Chapter 6*).

5.2.1: for loop

The syntax is:

```
for ( initialization, condition, increment ) {
    ......... code ...................
}
```

- o The **initialization** part initialize a **variable** and it executes ___only once___ in the **for loop** lifecycle.

- o The condition part contains a logical operation.

- o The increment part increments the **variable** and it executes ___every time___ after the block of code executes.

<u>**Execution flow of a for loop**</u>

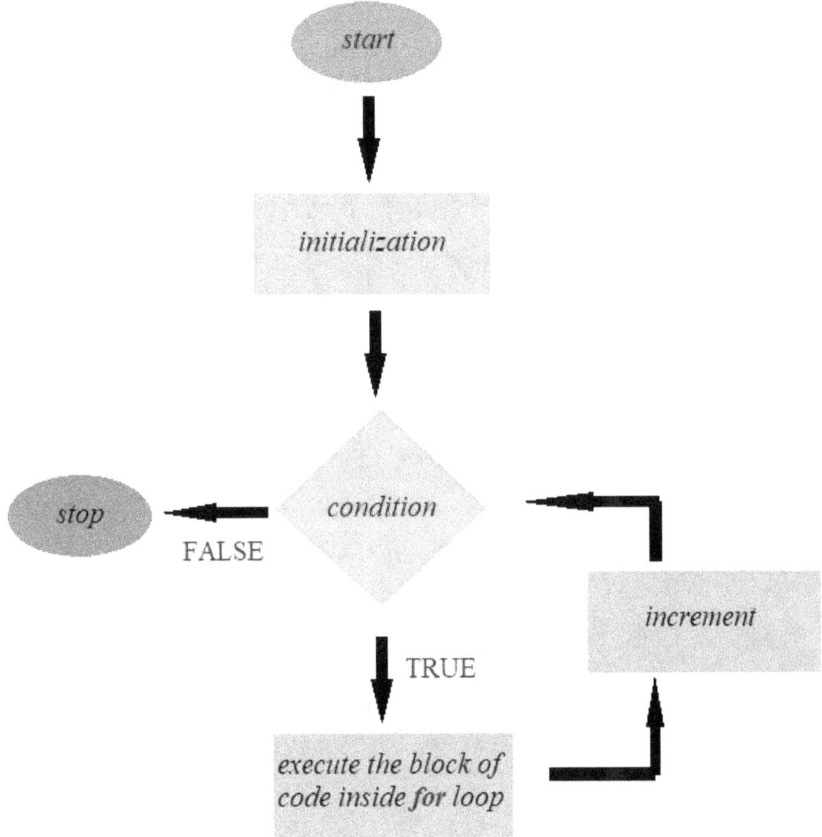

<u>**Example**</u>

- Launch **Eclipse IDE** and create a new **Class** *(I named my **class** Loops)*.

- Write the following lines of code in ***Loops.java***.

```java
1 package hello_world;
2
3 public class Loops {
4
5      public static void main(String[] args) {
6
7          for (int i = 0; i <= 5; i++) {
8              System.out.println(i);
9          }
10
11     }
12
13 }
```

Code explanation:

- At line 3, **class *Loops*** is declared.

- At line 5, the **main method** is written *(this line of code is discussed in chapter 3 and 4)*.

- At line 7, the **for loop** is stated.

  o In *initialization part,* the variable *i* is declared and a value of 0 is assigned to it.

  o In *condition part*, the condition of *i <= 5* is set.

  o In *increment part*, we increment the value of *i* by 1. The value of *i* will increment by 1 every time the condition is satisfied or returns **TRUE** and the block of code executes.

- At line 8, the value of *i* is printed.

Execution process of the above piece of code:

- $i = 0$ -> the condition is checked *(i is indeed less than 5, so the condition returns TRUE)* -> line 8 runs -> *i* is incremented 1.
  Present value of *i* is 1.

- $i = 1$ -> the condition is checked *(i is indeed less than 5, so the condition returns TRUE)* -> lines 8 runs -> *i* is incremented 1.
  Present value of *i* is 2.

- $i = 2$ -> the condition is checked *(i is indeed less than 5, so the condition returns TRUE)* -> lines 8 runs -> *i* is incremented 1.
  Present value of *i* is 3.

- $i = 3$ -> the condition is checked *(i is indeed less than 5, so the condition returns TRUE)* -> lines 8 runs -> *i* is incremented 1.
  Present value of *i* is 4.

- $i = 4$ -> the condition is checked *(i is indeed less than 5, so the condition returns TRUE)* -> lines 8 runs -> *i* is incremented 1.
  Present value of *i* is 5.

- $i = 5$ -> the condition is checked *(i is indeed equal to 5, so the condition returns TRUE)* -> lines 8 runs -> *i* is incremented 1.
  Present value of *i* is 6.

- $i = 6$ -> the condition is checked (*i* is NOT less than or equal to 5, so the condition is FALSE) -> EXIT out of the loop.

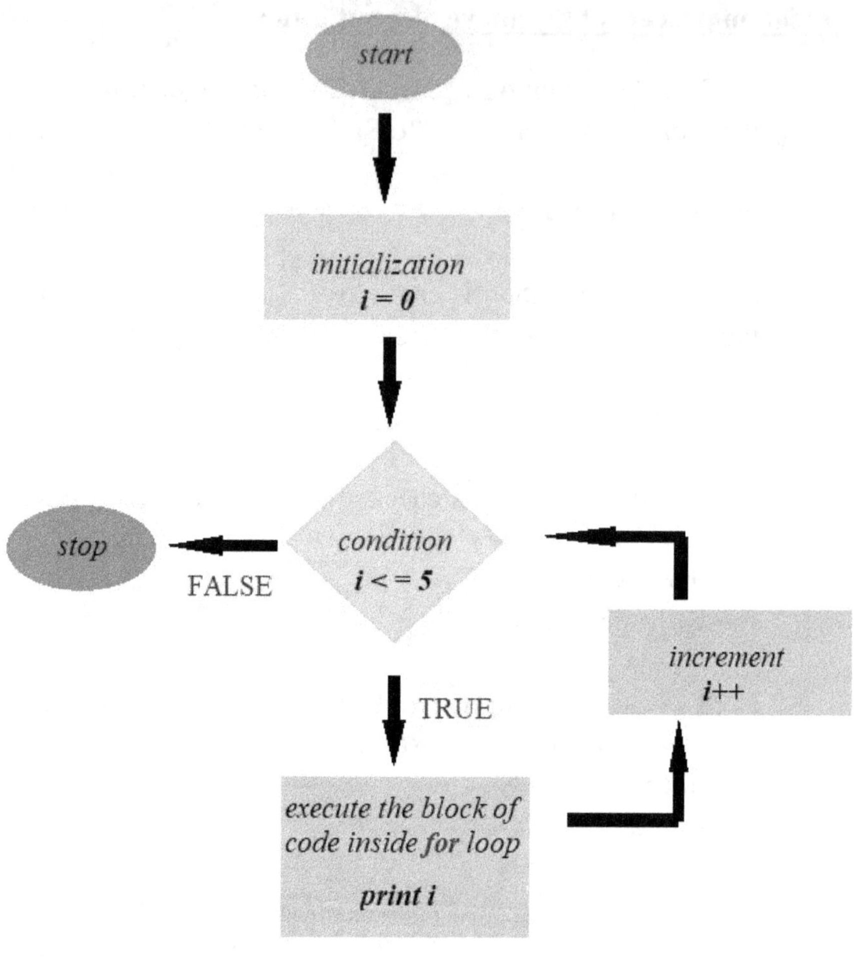

Now let's run the above piece of code:

5.2.2: <u>while loop</u>

while loop keeps on executing a block of code as long as the condition is **TRUE**.

The syntax is:

while (condition **) {**
..........*code*...............
}

<u>Example</u>

```java
 1  package hello_world;
 2
 3  public class Loops {
 4
 5      public static void main(String[] args) {
 6
 7          int i = 0;
 8
 9          while (i < 5) {
10              System.out.println(i);
11              i++;
12          }
13
14      }
15
16  }
```

Code explanation:

- At line 7, **instance variable** *(instance variable discussed in chapter 3, section 3.2)* *i* is declared and a value 0 is assigned to it.

- At line 9, **while loop** is declared with a **condition**. This loop will go on till the value of *i* is less than 5.

5.3: Break statement

Break statements are used to break out of a loop if certain condition is satisfied.

Example

➢ In **Eclipse IDE**, create a new **Class** *(I named my class BreakExample)*

```
1  package hello_world;
2
3  public class BreakExample {
4
5      public static void main(String[] args) {
6
7          System.out.println("Looking for number 3");
8
9          for (int i = 0; i <= 5; i++) {
10
11              if (i == 3) {
12                  System.out.println("Found 3, so exit the loop");
13                  break;
14              }
15
16              System.out.println("The number is " + i);
17          }
18
19      }
20
21  }
```

Execution flow of the above piece of code:

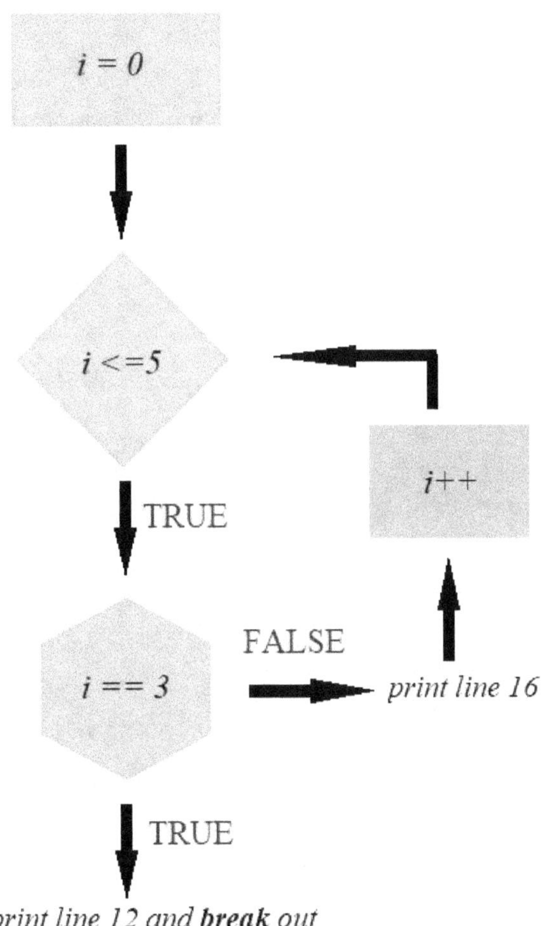

Chapter 6: Array

- An Array is a collection of elements all having the same **data type**.

- The syntax for Array declaration is:

    data_type[ ] *array_name*

    or

    data_type[ ] *array_name = { element1, element2 ....}*

    or

    data_type[ ] *array_name =* new **data_type[** *array size* **]**

Let us consider the *Fruits* category. *Fruits* can be divided into *apple*, *orange*, *banana*, *strawberry* etc.

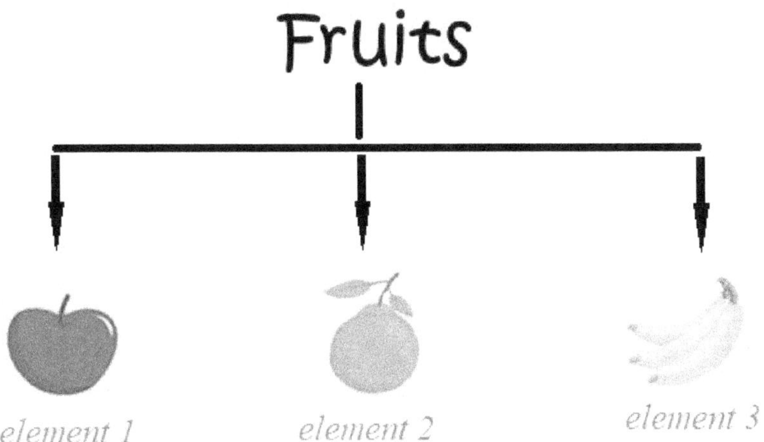

In **Java**, we can store all the fruits items or elements *(shown in the screen shot above)* into a single **variable** using **array**.

For example:
String[ ] fruits = { "apple", "orange", "banana" }

fruits is an **array** which holds or stores elements of **data type** String and *fruits* stores elements *apple*, *orange* and *banana*.

How to access any value from an Array?

- An **array** element can only be accessed from its **index value**.

- The syntax for accessing an element from an **array** is:
  array_name [index_value]

Index value	0	1	2
	apple	*orange*	*banana*

In the above *fruits* example, *apple* is present at **index value** 0. *orange* is present at **index value** 1 and *banana* is present at **index value** 2.

- In order to access *apple* from the *fruits* **array**, we need to write *fruits[0]*.
- In order to access *orange* from the *fruits* **array**, we need to write *fruits[1]*.
- In order to access *banana* from the *fruits* **array**, we need to write *fruits[2]*.

Please note: The index value always starts with 0.

Example 1

1. **Without using for loop**

➢ Launch **Eclipse IDE** -> create a new **Class** (*I named my class ArrayFruits*)

```java
1 package hello_world;
2
3 public class ArrayFruits {
4
5     public static void main(String[] args) {
6
7         String[] fruits = { "apple", "orange", "banana" };
8
9         System.out.println(fruits[0]);
10         System.out.println(fruits[1]);
11         System.out.println(fruits[2]);
12
13     }
14
15 }
```

Now let's run the above piece of code:

2. Using for loop

(for loop discussed in chapter 5)

```java
1 package hello_world;
2
3 public class ArrayFruits {
4
5     public static void main(String[] args) {
6
7         String[] fruits = { "apple", "orange", "banana" };
8
9         for (int i = 0; i < fruits.length; i++) {
10             System.out.println(fruits[i]);
11         }
12
13     }
14
15 }
```

Code explanation:

- In line 9, you will notice the **condition** $i < fruits.length$;

<table>
<tr><td>

What is length?

length is a special **variable** which returns the length of an **array**. In this example, the length of **array** *fruits* is 3 because it contains 3 elements *apple, orange* and *banana*.

</td></tr>
</table>

This **condition** states to continue the **for loop** till *i* is less than the **length** of the **array**. Since the **length** of the **array** is 3, the **for loop** will loop 3 times.

<u>**Execution flow of the above piece of code:**</u>

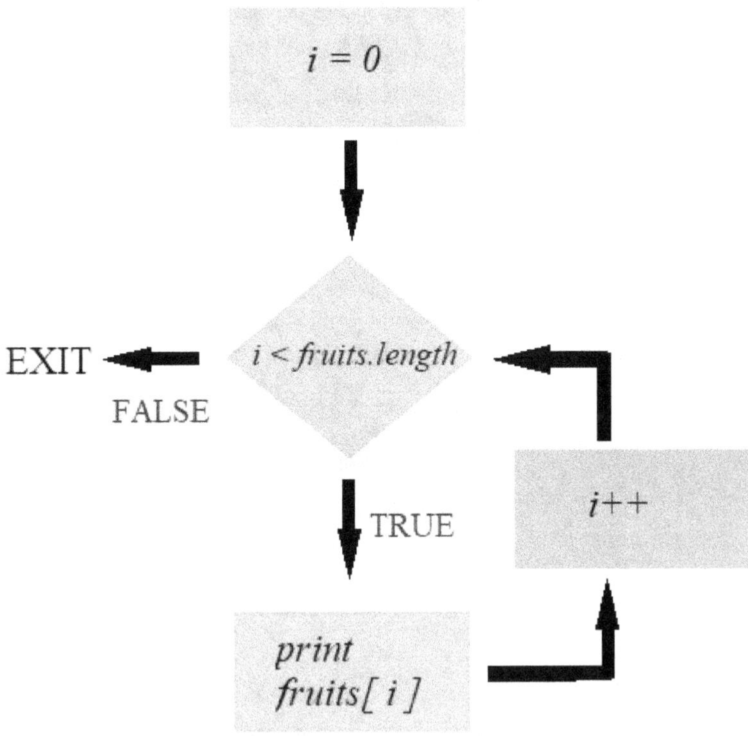

<u>**Example 2**</u>

 ➢ Let's create another **class** (I named my *class Car*)

```java
1 package hello_world;
2
3 public class Car {
4
5     String[] show = new String[2];
6
7     public String[] car_info(String make, String model) {
8
9         show[0] = make;
10         show[1] = model;
11         return show;
12     }
13
14     public static void main(String[] args) {
15
16         Car c = new Car();
17
18         String[] x = c.car_info("Ford", "F2021");
19
20         for (int i = 0; i < x.length; i++) {
21             System.out.println(x[i]);
22         }
23
24     }
25
26 }
```

Code explanation:

- At line 5, we declared an **array *show*** whose **data type** is **string**. We also set its *size* meaning that this **array** will only hold 2 elements.

- At line 7, we declared a **method *car_info*** with two **parameters *make*** and ***model*.**
  *(*This method will **return** an **array** of **data type string***)*.

  o At line 9, we store ***make*** at **array** position 0.

  o At line 10, we store ***model*** at **array** position 1.

o   At line 11, we **return** the **array *show***.

- At line 18, we access the ***car_info* method** and pass values into it.
  car_info* returns** an **array** of **data type string** and that result gets stored in another **array *x.

- From line 20 to 21, we print out the elements from **array *x***.

Let's run the above piece of code:

```
Problems   @ Javadoc   Declaration   Console
<terminated> Car [Java Application] C:\eclipse\eclipse\plugins\o
Ford
F2021
```

> **Please note:** In order to **return** multiple values from a **method**, we can use **array** as we did in above example.

Chapter 7: Object Oriented Programming Concepts

The most important Object Oriented Programming or OOP concepts are:-
1. Encapsulation
2. Inheritance
3. Polymorphism

7.1: Encapsulation

*   Encapsulation is the mechanism in which all the **Java methods** and **variable** are wrapped up into a single unit *(***Class***)*.

Class

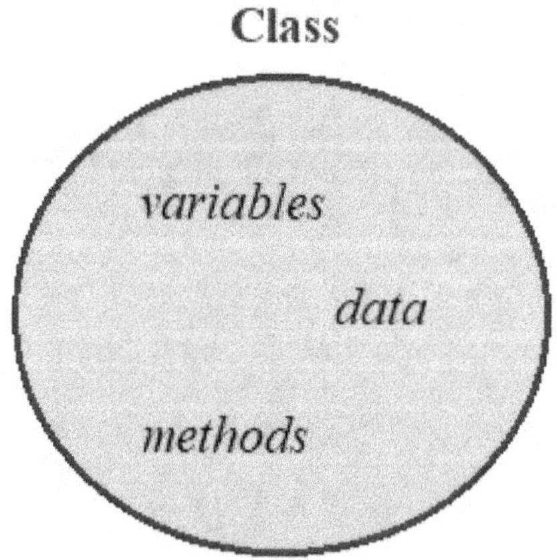

*   Encapsulation helps to protect the data present inside the unit and prevents any malicious activity.

- In Encapsulation, the **variables** of a **class** is declared **private** *(private access modifiers explained in chapter 3, section 3.4).*
  In order to access the **private variable** from outside the **class**, **get** and **set methods** are used.
  set method is used to set a value and **get method** is used to get the value.

Example

> Launch **Eclipse IDE** -> create a new **Class** *(I named my class Encap).*

```
1  package hello_world;
2
3  public class Encap {
4
5      private String username;
6      private String password;
7
8
9  }
```

In **Encap class**, I declared two **variables** *username* and *password*.
Since both *username* and *password* carries very important and sensitive data *(sensitive data are those data which must be hidden and protected at any cost),* so we declared its **access modifier** as **private** meaning that no **class** outside *Encap* **class** can access these **variables**. In order to access these **private variables**, we need **get** and **set methods**.

> To generate **get** and **set methods** of **variables** *username* and *password*, click on the yellow bulb like icon beside *username*

and ***password*** and select *Create getter and setter for 'username'* and *Create getter and setter for 'password'* respectively.

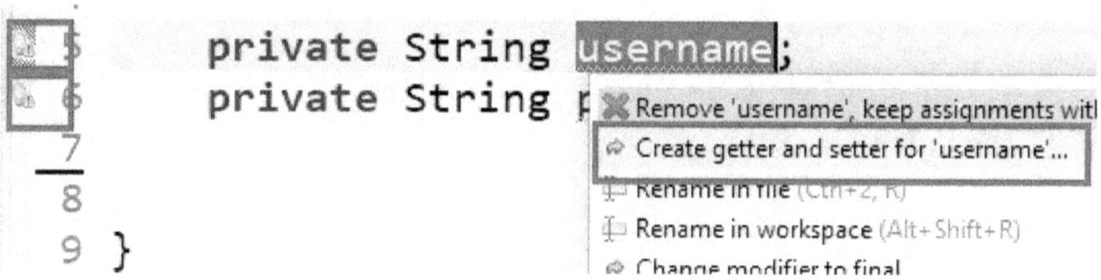

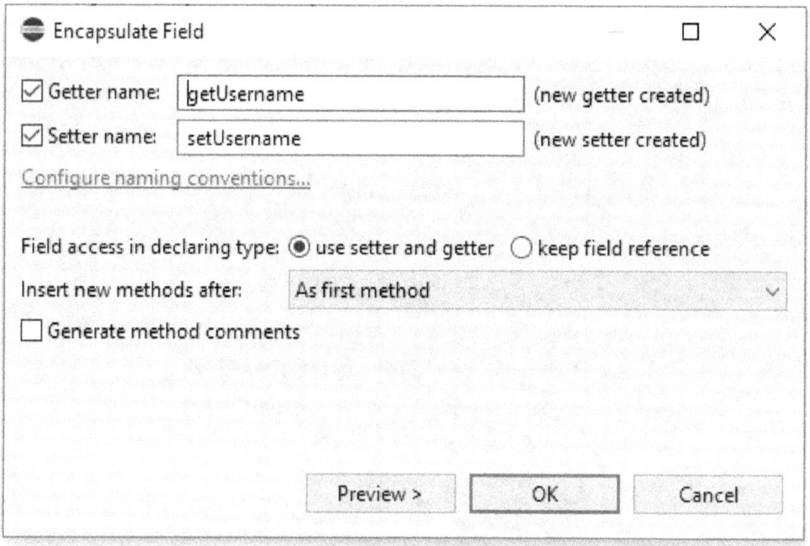

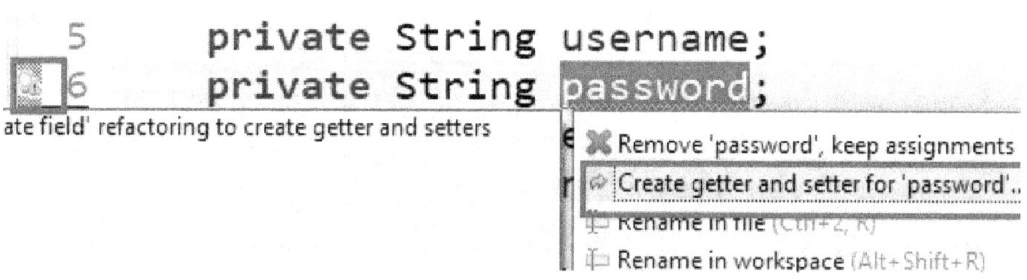

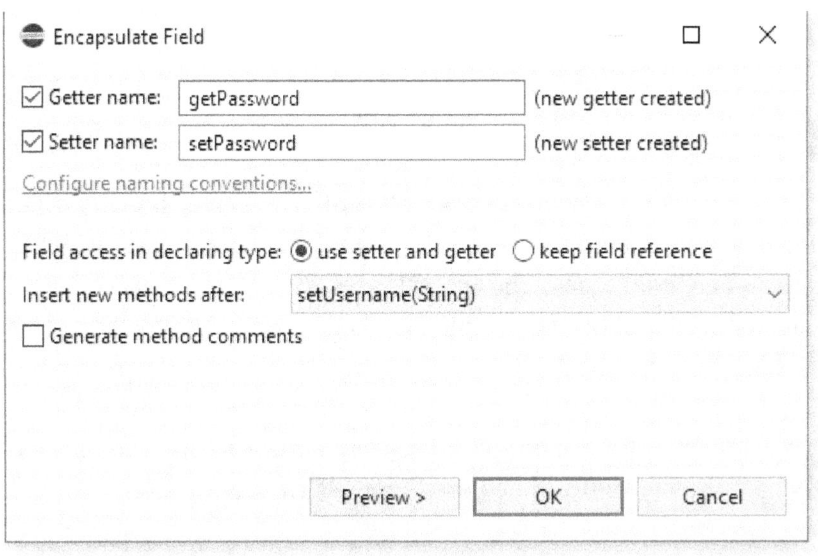


```java
1  package hello_world;
2
3  public class Encap {
4
5      private String username;
6      private String password;
7      public String getUsername() {
8          return username;
9      }
10     public void setUsername(String username) {
11         this.username = username;
12     }
13     public String getPassword() {
14         return password;
15     }
16     public void setPassword(String password) {
17         this.password = password;
18     }
```

In the above example, **Class *Encap*** is **public** meaning that any other **class** can access **Class *Encap*** but its **variables** are **private** meaning no other **class** can access these **variables** except for **Class *Encap*.** The **get** and **set** **methods** are **public** meaning that any other **class** can access these **methods**.

➤ Let's create another **class** *(I named my class Encap2)* and access the **get** and **set** **method** declared in **class *Encap*.**

```java
1  package hello_world;
2
3  public class Encap2 {
4
5      public static void main(String[] args) {
6          Encap e = new Encap();
7
8          e.setUsername("John");
9          System.out.println(e.getUsername());
10
11         e.setPassword("J123");
12         System.out.println(e.getPassword());
13
14     }
15
16 }
```

Code explanation:

▪ Since **Class *Encap*** was **public**, **Class *Encap2*** can access it easily.

In line 6, an **object** of **class *Encap*** is created and its **set** and **get methods** are accessed.

*First we pass a value to **variable username** using its **set method** at line 8 and then we get and print out the value using its **get method** at line 9.*
*Then we pass a value to **variable password** using its **set method** at line11 and then we get and print out the value using its **get method** at line 12.*

Let's run the above piece of code:

```
Problems   @ Javadoc   Declaration   Console
<terminated> Encap2 [Java Application] C:\eclipse\eclipse\plugi
John
J123
```

7.2: Inheritance

Important points to note are:

- Inheritance is a mechanism in which a **subclass** or **child class** inherits all the properties from **superclass** or **parent class**.

- The main usage of Inheritance is code reusability.

- The **subclass** or **child class** inherits properties from its **parent class** using **extends keyword**.

```
class Parent {
................code...........
}
class Child extends Parent {
..................code...............
}
```

- A **subclass** can contain its own properties as well as its **parent class** properties.

Example: Let us consider a school district **XYZ** contains three schools, *elementary school*, *middle school* and *high school* and all the three schools are built on the same street and on the same location. The common attribute between these schools are:

1. They all are schools or educational institution.
2. They all are built on the same street but have different building names and numbers.
3. They all fall under the same school district.

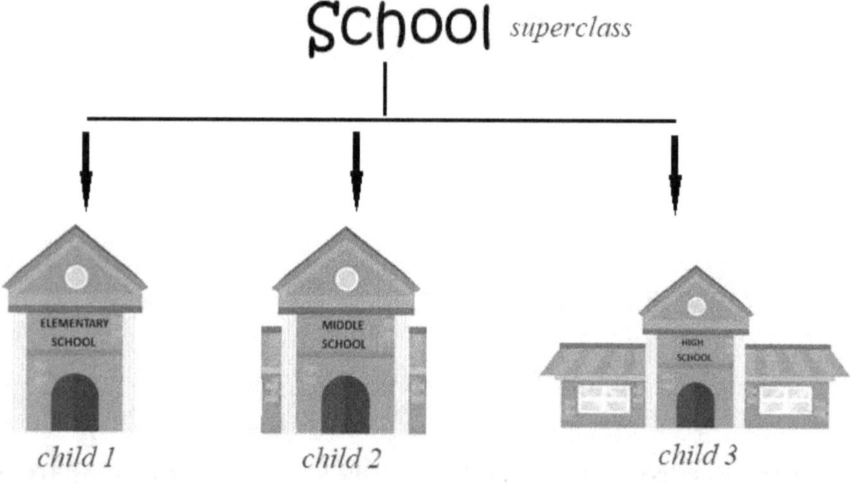

child 1   child 2   child 3

While coding, instead of writing these common information for each school again and again, we can write them once in a single place *(in a superclass or parent class)* and call them whenever any other **class** needs them.

Example

➤ Launch **Eclipse IDE**, create a new **class** *(I named my class SchoolSuperClass)* and this **class** will act as a **superclass**.

➤ Create three more **classes**, one for *elementary school (I named my class ElementaryChild)*, one for *middle school (I named my class MiddleChild)* and one for *high school (I named my class HighChild)*. These three **classes** will act as a **child class** of superclass *SchoolSuperClass.java*.

➤ In **superclass** *SchoolSuperClass.java,* write the following lines of code:

```
 1 package hello_world;
 2
 3 public class SchoolSuperClass {
 4
 5     String schoolId;
 6     int building_num;
 7
 8     public void street_address() {
 9         System.out.println("The street address is XYZ");
10     }
11 }
```

In this **class**, we declared all the **variables** and **methods** which are common to all three schools.

• Open *ElementaryChild.java,* and write the following lines of code

```java
1 package hello_world;
2
3 public class ElementaryChild extends SchoolSuperClass {
4
5°     public static void main(String[] args) {
6
7         ElementaryChild e = new ElementaryChild();
8
9         e.schoolId = "E123";
10         e.building_num = 222;
11
12         System.out.println(e.schoolId);
13         System.out.println(e.building_num);
14         e.street_address();
15     }
16
17 }
```

Code explanation:

- At line 3, with the help of **extends keyword**, all properties of superclass *SchoolSuperClass* are incorporated into **child class** *ElementaryChild.*

- At line 7, **object *e*** of *ElementaryChild* **class** is created.

- At line 9 and line 10, the **variables** *school_Id* and *building_num* are accessed from **superclass** and values are passed into it.

- At line 12 and 13, the values of the **variables** are printed.

- At line 14, the *street_address( )* **method** present in **superclass** is called.

Now let's run the above piece of code:

- Open the second **class** file ***MiddleChild.java*** and write the following lines of code:

```
1 package hello_world;
2
3 public class MiddleChild extends SchoolSuperClass {
4
5     public static void main(String[] args) {
6         MiddleChild m = new MiddleChild();
7
8         m.schoolId = "M678";
9         m.building_num = 225;
10
11         System.out.println(m.schoolId);
12         System.out.println(m.building_num);
13         m.street_address();
14
15     }
16
17 }
```

*The above piece of code is very similar to **ElementaryChild.java**, only data is different.*

Let's run the above piece of code:

81

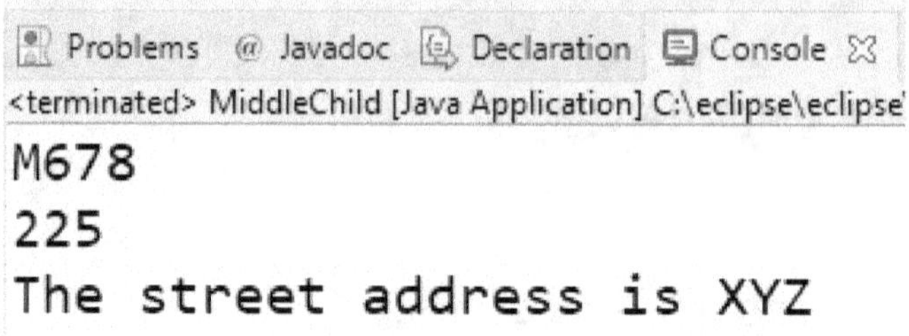

We followed the same process above for *HighChild.java.*

7.3: Polymorphism

Polymorphism is a mechanism in which a **method** can be executed in many forms based on the **object** that is acting upon it.

Polymorphism is of 2 types:

1. Dynamic Polymorphism or Run Time polymorphism
2. Static Polymorphism or Compile time polymorphism

7.3.1: Dynamic Polymorphism

The most important example of this type of Polymorphism is **Method overriding**.

- When **superclass** and **subclass** have **method** with same name and **signature**, the **method** of the **subclass** tends to overrides the **method** of the **superclass**. This mechanism is called **Method overriding**.

- When **method** of the **superclass** and **subclass** have same method *(with same name and signature)*, the **compiler** does not understand which **method** to execute. This type of conflict is resolved at **run time** and due to this **Dynamic Polymorphism** is also called **Run time polymorphism**.

<u>Example</u>

Let's create a **Method overriding** scenario.

> Launch **Eclipse IDE** and create a new **Superclass** *(I named my class Animal)*

```
1 package hello_world;
2
3 public class Animal {
4
5      public void eat() {
6          System.out.println("Animals eat veg or non-veg");
7      }
8
9 }
```

> Create two **subclasses** *(I named one **subclass Cow** and other subclass Lion)*

```java
1 package hello_world;
2
3 public class Cow extends Animal {
4
5     public void eat() {
6         System.out.println("Cows eat grass");
7     }
8
9     public static void main(String[] args) {
10        Animal c = new Cow();
11        c.eat();
12
13    }
14
15 }
```



```java
1 package hello_world;
2
3 public class Lion extends Animal {
4
5     public void eat() {
6         System.out.println("Lions eat meat");
7     }
8
9     public static void main(String[] args) {
10        Animal l = new Lion();
11        l.eat();
12
13    }
14
15 }
```

Superclass *Animal* have an *eat* **method** and both **subclasses** *Cow* and *Lion* also have the same **method** with same name and **signature** *(highlighted in the screen shot above)* .

In **Class** *Cow.java*, at line 10, we created **object** *c* of **type** *Animal* and a call was made to the *Cow* **constructor**.
At line 11, we called the *eat* **method**.

After running *Cow.java* we get an output of

In **Class** *Lion.java*, at line 10, we created **object** *l* of **type** *Animal* and a call was made to the *Lion* **constructor**.
At line 11, we called the *eat* **method**.

After running *Lion.java* we get an output of

In both cases we see that the *eat* **method** of each **subclass** *(Cow and Lion)* overrides the *eat* **method** of **superclass** *(Animal).*

7.3.2: Static Polymorphism

The most important example of this type of Polymorphism is **Method Overloading**.

- In **Method Overloading**, a **class** can contain multiple **methods** with same name with different **signature**.

- **Static Polymorphism** is also called **Compile time Polymorphism** because in this case the **compiler** knows which **method** to execute based on the **method signature** and the conflict is resolved at compile time.

Example

> Launch **Eclipse IDE** -> create a new **class** *(I named my class SPExample)*

```java
1  package hello_world;
2
3  public class SPExample {
4
5      public void show() {
6          System.out.println("Hi");
7      }
8
9      public void show(String name) {
10         System.out.println("Hello, " + name);
11     }
12
13     public static void main(String[] args) {
14         SPExample s = new SPExample();
15         s.show();
16         s.show("Katy");
17
18     }
19
20 }
```

Code explanation:

- At line 5, a **method** named *show* is declared.

- At line 9, another **method** named *show* is declared with a **parameter**.
- At line 15, *show( )* **method** is called.

- At line 16, the other *show( )* **method** is called and an **argument** is passed into it.

Now let's run the above piece of code.

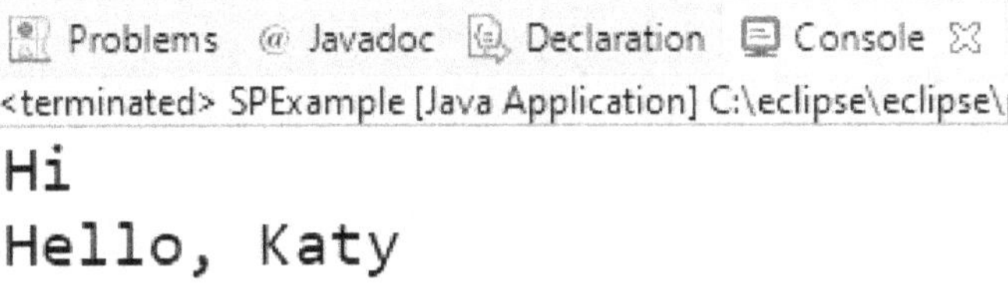

In the above example, we see there are two **methods**, both have the same name (*show*) but have different **signature** *(one without parameter and other with parameter)* .
When we run the above piece of code, it runs perfectly because the **compiler** was able to distinguish between the two **methods** based on their **signature**.

TEST

1. Write a program which will print **even** and **odd** numbers from 1 to 10.

    *When a number is divided by 2, if its remainder returns 0, then the number is **even**.*
    *When a number is divided by 2, if its remainder does not returns 0, then the number is **odd**.*

2. Write a program that will loop through an **array** and will *break* out of the loop once a condition is satisfied.

    Given: Array car *containing 5 elements Toyota, Kia, Ford, Tesla, Truck.*
    *Exit out of the loop once **car** is equal to Tesla.*

3. Write a program which will contain two **methods** with **parameters** and these **methods** will *return* values once called and **arguments** are passed into it.

    *Method 1 should return an **integer** result after performing arithmetic **multiply** operation.*
    *Method 2 should return an **integer** result after performing arithmetic **division** operation.*

4. Write a program which will contain one **method** with a **parameter** and this **method** will **return** the result once called and an **argument** is passed into it.

    *The method much have a **parameter** whose data type is **string** and this method must **return** the **string** value once called and an **argument** is passed into it.*

Answers

1.

```
 1  package hello_world;
 2
 3  public class Test1 {
 4
 5      public static void main(String[] args) {
 6
 7          for (int i = 1; i <= 10; i++) {
 8
 9              if (i % 2 == 0) {
10                  System.out.println("Even number: " + i);
11              } else {
12                  System.out.println("Odd number: " + i);
13              }
14          }
15
16      }
17
18  }
```

2.

```
package hello_world;

public class Test2 {

    public static void main(String[] args) {

        String[] car = { "Toyota", "Kia", "Ford", "Tesla", "Truck" };

        for (int i = 0; i < car.length; i++) {

            if (car[i] == "Tesla") {
                System.out.println("I wish to own Tesla one day");
                break;
            }
            System.out.println("Tesla not found, loop no. " + i);
        }

    }

}
```

3.

```java
package hello_world;

public class Test3 {
    int z;

    public int multiply(int x, int y) {
        z = x * y;
        return z;
    }

    public int division(int x, int y) {
        z = x / y;
        return z;
    }

    public static void main(String[] args) {
        Test3 t3 = new Test3();
        System.out.println(t3.multiply(20, 10));
        System.out.println(t3.division(15, 4));

    }

}
```

4.

```java
package hello_world;

public class Test4 {

    public String name(String name) {
        return name;
    }

    public static void main(String[] args) {

        Test4 t4 = new Test4();
        System.out.println("My name is " + t4.name("Basu"));

    }

}
```

Wish you all the best and thank you very much for buying this book.

Always remember, the most important learning is Self-Learning..